VICTORIA CALLIHOO
An Amazing Life

The Publisher: Eschia Books Inc.

Library and Archives Canada Cataloguing in Publication

Taylor, Cora, 1936–
Victoria Callihoo : an amazing life / by Cora Taylor.

Includes bibliographical references.
ISBN 978-0-9810942-4-3

1. Callihoo, Victoria, 1861–1966. 2. Métis women—Alberta—
Biography. 3. Women hunters—Alberta—Biography. 4. Frontier
and pioneer life—Alberta. 5. Sainte Anne, Lac (Alta.)—Biography.
6. Alberta—Biography. I. Title.

FC109.1.C33T39 2009   971.23'3004970092   C2009-900204-3

Project Director and Editor:
Kathy van Denderen
Cover Design:
Joy Dirto
Cover Image:
Courtesy of: Library of Congress Print and Photographs
Division (3C02039, 3C03498) and Photos.com
Illustrator:
Peter Tyler (p. 119)

Photo Credits:
Every effort has been made to accurately credit the sources of photographs.
Any errors or omissions should be reported directly to the publisher for
correction in future editions. Photographs courtesy of Cora Taylor (p. 67),
Glenbow Archives (p. 134, NA-47-9; p. 140, NA-1592-1), Musée Héritage
Museum and Archives, St. Albert (pp. 32–34, p. 89), Provincial Archives
of Alberta (p. 12, PR1979.0269.72d; pp. 55–58, OB8575, OB8555, OB8563,
OB1085; p. 79, OB540; p. 86, BP2.11197).

PC:1

VICTORIA CALLIHOO
An Amazing Life

CORA TAYLOR

ESCHIA
BOOKS

Contents

*This book is dedicated to all those amazing
women, like Victoria Callihoo,
whose stories haven't been told.*

Thank you.

Acknowledgements

I WOULD LIKE to thank the Alberta Foundation for the Arts for a grant to begin work on this project.

I am grateful to the people who communicated with me and helped with the information I needed: Janice MacDonald and Carrielynn Lund who were there helping me at the beginning. Thanks to Naomi McIlwraith of the Faculty of Native Studies at the University of Alberta who generously shared her pemmican experience with me. I cannot adequately express my gratitude to Professor Robert A. Papen, Departement de Linguistique et de Didactique des Langues, Université du Québec à Montréal, who interrupted his Mexican holiday to go over my efforts on the Michif language—any mistakes are mine!

What would I do without friends—especially Dr. Nancy Gibson, who's given me support and advice and a trip around Lac Ste. Anne, Alberta Beach and Onoway; to Martina Purdon for her support and advice and letting me know about Jack Brink's wonderful book; and Merle Harris, always there with support and for introducing me to Naomi McIlwraith.

Thank you to Hugh Dempsey, editor of *Alberta History* (formerly *Alberta Historical Review*) for kind permission to reprint the Victoria Callihoo articles, and to Debbie Goodine of the Alberta Historical Society for her assistance.

So many people helped me track down the material I needed: Diane Lamoureux, Oblate Archivist at the Provincial Archives of Alberta, and Katie Roth and Karen Simonson at the Archives as well; Harry Saunders and Jim Bowman at the Glenbow Archives; Tim Atherton, Sharon Morin, Selina Loyer and Sherry Strachan at the Musée Héritage Museum in St. Albert; Sylvia McGinley and the Alberta Beach Museum; and Helen Thornitt and Yvonne Slemko at the Onoway Museum who gave me information and names of people to contact.

Thank you to the people at Eschia Books for welcoming this book and steering it to publication.

Last but not least as they say, to my husband, Earl Georgas, who put up with my 2:00 AM writing when the deadlines were looming—thank you!

Introduction

WHEN I FIRST THOUGHT of writing this book, the bits of memoir Victoria Callihoo left behind fascinated me. Although I never met her, I heard of her when I first moved to Edmonton in 1961, although by then she was an old woman. She died in 1966 at the age of 104.

In one of my first books for Penguin's Our Canadian Girl series, *Angelique: The Buffalo Hunt*, I gratefully acknowledged Victoria's story in *Alberta Historical Review* for some of the details in the book.

Later, when I was working on the Social Studies book (*Alberta: Many People*) for Pearson Educational Publishers, I wrote a short bio on Victoria, though it was not included. Still, this woman's life, which had gone from the time of the Red River cart and the last of the great herds of Plains bison to jet planes and computers, intrigued me.

When I read about her connection to the Iroquois voyageurs on the one side of her family and the famous John Rowand of Fort Edmonton, she seemed to me to be some kind of western Canadian royalty. After all, didn't author Jim MacGregor call Rowand the "Czar of the Prairies"? And wasn't Victoria named after the young Queen Victoria? Indeed, I learned that later in her life as matriarch of the Callihoo clan, she was lovingly referred to as "Queen Victoria," too.

Although anyone living 104 years might be able to claim to have experienced amazing changes, Victoria's life was remarkable, too, because of the picture it draws of the development of the Métis nation in western Canada. She epitomized the growth of a new people and the way they adapted to the changing world of the 19th and 20th centuries.

The Métis were not afraid to follow the lifestyle of their Native ancestors in the buffalo hunts and to use pemmican as a food staple, but they added the mix of their French/European ancestry as well. Their inventiveness was shown in the creation of their own dance, the Red River jig—something at which Victoria excelled. In addition, the Métis of western Canada created a distinctive new language, Michif. But all the time that the Métis nation was growing around her, Victoria was working hard and raising a family, just as women in her circumstances have always done. Studying her life is a wonderful opportunity to follow our Alberta history.

Chapter One

Background—
Lac Ste. Anne

Long before Victoria was born, before the voyageurs came to northwestern Alberta with the fur traders, there was the lake. The Cree called the lake *Manitou Sakahigan*, which translates as Spirit Lake. The Nakota Sioux, who lived on the west end of the lake, called it *Wakamne*, or God's Lake.

These First Nations people believed the water could heal the sick, and it was a tradition for centuries for them to gather there each year. In fact, archaeological evidence has been found that indicates the early people inhabited the area as far back as 5000 to 6000 years ago.[1]

Early traders translated the name as Devil's Lake because of the sudden storms that would rise up and swamp their boats. It was not unusual for a summer squall to catch boaters off guard because the lake is large enough to be dangerous even with motorized boats today.

When the missionaries followed the fur trade to western Canada, the lake was renamed Lac Ste. Anne. Saint Anne, who was the mother of the Virgin Mary, was said to have been seen standing on a rock in the lake during a storm in the mid-1800s. Her footprints could be seen on a stone underwater near the old church.[2] Saint Anne, the missionaries said, gave the lake water healing properties. In July 1844, Father Jean-Baptiste Thibault, robed in stole and surplice, blessed the lake and named it Lac Ste. Anne.[3]

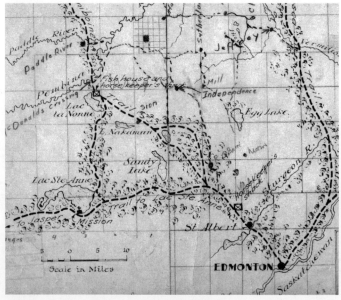

Area northwest of Fort Edmonton (1883)

By this time, some of the area around the lake was settled by the families of French and Iroquois voyageurs. They had came west with the fur traders and had married women from Cree and other tribes. The men were not called "voyageurs" in those days but *engagés,* referring to their being hired on as employees. The North West Company and Hudson's Bay Company (HBC) referred to these men as "servants." The men had signed contracts in eastern Canada to work for the HBC for two years. They worked 20-hour days, paddling canoes and hauling packs. Where the rivers and rapids were too dangerous, they would *portage,* which meant carrying the heavy loads on their backs.

Life for the voyageurs was hard. Living in the outdoors and long hours of paddling the freighter canoes had toughened them. They came upriver, paddling hard against the current with loads of supplies and trade goods. They travelled on the river system between Montréal and the North Saskatchewan River that brought them to the forts in western Canada.

The canoes were much bigger than any you might see today. Some were as large as 36 feet long and 6 feet wide and would carry five tons of trade goods. The "north" canoe, as it was called, was smaller but was still around 28 feet long and 4 or 5 feet wide with a crew of 8 or 10 men. The main paddlers were known as "middlemen"—they sat in the middle of the canoe and provided the power. It was considered a reward for good work for a man to be promoted to steersman at the back of the canoe.

The canoes were heavily loaded with iron pots, blankets, coats, tobacco, traps, axes, saws, knives, guns and ammunition to trade for furs. Kegs of rum or brandy as well as other items, such as needles, mirrors, silver ornaments, oatmeal, sugar, oilcloth and lime juice, were also on the canoes for the use of the traders and others employed at the forts.

Returning downstream was easier for the voyageurs, but that was also when the canoes were loaded even more heavily. They were laden with bales of tightly packed furs of beaver, muskrat, otter and other animals the Native trappers had brought to the forts to trade.

Bales weighed exactly 90 pounds whether they contained furs or trade goods, though the size varied with the latter depending on what was being brought to the western forts. This weight was strictly adhered to—it was a clever plan by the fur traders because any pilfering was recognized by the lightness of the load![4] During portages, each voyageur carried two bales, often more. A Mistassini named Chief Solomon Voyageur is said to have carried the equivalent of eight packs over a half-mile stretch.[5] That would have been 720 pounds! It's not known what the terrain was like during Chief Solomon's journey, but most portages involved very rough country—usually uphill from the river or lake, over slippery rocks or through thick brush.

It is easy to understand why these "canoe men" would rather brave dangerous rapids than have to unload their canoes and carry them across country.

But some of these men did not return east. Although their contracts called for them to end their two years as "servants" of the HBC back in eastern Canada, once their time was up they were known as "freemen." Many of them did not return to eastern Canada but preferred to settle in the West. Work was always available near the trading posts, and the men could hunt and fish for food and trap furs to trade at the fort.

It was a challenge to keep food supplied year-round, but by this time many of the men had met and started families with women from local tribes or mixed-blood daughters of other men connected with the fur trade.

And if the men were used to a hard life, their Native wives were just as capable. Often it was the women who knew the country best. Women frequently trapped and skinned animals to supply their families with meat. They also tanned the animal hides and sewed them into clothing.

These women knew the country and often guided the men on hunting parties away from the rivers. In earlier times they interpreted and formed a relationship between the fur traders and the local tribes that helped to avoid conflict at the trading posts.

Alexander Mackenzie recognized the value of the Native women's expertise. In 1786 he complained, "I do not have a single one in my fort who can make *rackets* (snowshoes). I do not know what to do without these articles. See what it is to have no wives."[6]

During the buffalo hunts it was the women who skinned the buffalo and dried the strips of meat that were pounded into a powdery form to prepare pemmican. This mixture of dried meat and berries and fat was then kept in animal skin bags to be eaten as needed. The bags were easy to carry, and the fur traders soon realized that pemmican was valuable. Native wives of the fort employees were kept busy preparing pemmican that the voyageurs ate when they had no time to hunt or when game was scarce in the country they travelled through.

When Napoleon said that his army "travelled on its stomach," he meant that without a food supply the army couldn't leave home. The tribes of the western plains had solved this problem by making pemmican. The people of the tribes could eat the mixture as it was when on the move, or they could boil it into a sort of stew called rababoo. Perhaps it wasn't everyone's idea of a tasty treat, but it was nourishing, and quick and easy to prepare—it was the "fast food" of those days.

Settlements at Lac Ste. Anne and St. Albert were set up when Oblate missionaries founded missions in the area. In 1843 Father Thibeault began the mission at Lac Ste. Anne.[7]

Some of the Iroquois freemen lived near *Fort des Prairies,* as they called Fort Edmonton. They hunted buffalo and trapped other animals for trade, then moved to settle near the fort. Among the people to settle there were the Belcourt and Callihoo families. But according to the records of the early missionaries, the HBC did not wish to have agricultural settlements near the forts because it would frighten away the fur-bearing animals.[8] Lac Ste. Anne was 50 miles from the fort so Father Thibeault felt it was far enough away from the jurisdiction of Chief Factor John Rowand and yet close enough for the men who settled there to be able to trade.

Lord Southesk described these men in the journals that he wrote while he was travelling in the area. "These hunters are fine looking men; dressed either in the usual fringed leather hunting shirts, or in blue cloth capots. Their caps are of blue cloth, small with a leather shade, and covered with streamers of ribbon, chiefly black blue and red."[9]

The "capots" Lord Southesk referred to in his writings were the *capotes,* or coats made from the blankets sold at the trading posts. They looked something like today's parka but came to the knees and were tied at the waist with a fringed sash. The Assomption sashes, or *ceinture fléchée,* were named after the weavers of L'Assumption, Québec, and were almost a trademark of those involved in the fur trade.[10] The Métis developed their own version of this colourful sash.

The Iroquois men brought little of their own culture with them, instead adapting to that of their Cree wives. By the 1850s these former voyageurs had lost their language and spoke a mixture of Cree and French.[11] The language created in this way is known today as Michif.

Chapter Two

Baby Girl

NOVEMBER 1861 WAS COLD, and the winds from Lac Ste. Anne whistled around Victoria's parents' little log cabin. But no matter how much the storms raged outside, the little family was warm and safe inside the cabin.

Victoria's father, Alexis Belcourt, had built the cabin. The walls were made out of spruce logs that had been well chinked with clay, and any bits that washed away with the summer rains were repaired well before the winter storms came again.

When you first came in from outside, the single-room cabin seemed dark. Two windows provided light to the room, but there was no glass for windowpanes, so the skin of a deer or moose calf was used to cover them. After the hair was scraped off the hide, and while it was still wet, it was nailed to slats around the window. When it dried, the hide stretched thin and tight, and although you couldn't see out the opening, it let in the daylight and kept out the wind, rain and snow.

But light also came from the mud stoves in the cabin. These were open fireplaces made of mud and dried grasses and were built in each corner of the room opposite the door. Blazing logs not only added light to the room but also kept the inhabitants warm.

When the mud stoves were being built, iron bars were set in before the mud was baked hard. The bars might have been obtained from the fort or the metal barrels of discarded guns. A kettle or a cooking pot was always hanging from the iron bars. The boiling water in the kettle could be made into tea at a moment's notice. And when the pot was suspended above the fire, the aroma of stew or soup filled the room.

The cabin had only one room, but it didn't seem cluttered even for a big family because there were no tables, chairs or beds. At night they spread buffalo robes out on the floor to sleep on. During the day, the robes were folded or rolled up and put against the walls.

Baby Victoria Anne was born on November 19, 1861. Her mother, Nancy Kinninawas Rowand, was a Cree medicine woman but she probably had another woman from the settlement come to help with the birth.

Victoria was the fifth of 11 children. When she was born, there were already four other little Belcourts. Twelve-year-old Sophie was the eldest, and she was a big help to her mother, caring for her two younger sisters, Christianne, who was six, and Louisa aged three. Sophie was excited to have a new baby girl in the family, even if it meant helping look after another little sister. Victoria had a big brother, too. Alexander was nine when she was born, old enough to help his father. A boy learned at a young age how to help the family survive, and Alexander already had his own little trapline.

He learned to hang loops of wire above the rabbit trails in the snow in the thick bush close to the family's cabin. Each morning he checked to see if a rabbit rushing through the bush had been caught. Sometimes he had to look at his trapline twice because the white winter coat of the rabbits blended so well with the snow. If a rabbit had been caught the previous evening, it would be frozen stiff, and had to be thawed before it could be skinned and the meat used.[1]

Tender rabbit meat tasted better than chicken. And Nancy could use the fur to trim clothes. First, of course, the skin was stretched and dried on a piece of wood that young Alexander had whittled into the right shape. Sophie had her own trapline, too—girls had to learn to provide food for the home as well.

Victoria's mother might want to use some of that soft rabbit fur in the hammock where baby Victoria spent the first few months of her life. She would be warm and cosy there, bundled up in a blanket hanging from the ceiling of the cabin. She was a real rock-a-bye baby!

No diapers were needed for the new baby; dried moss was used. The first disposable diaper! Better than Pampers, the moss not only kept the baby dry, it also absorbed the odour. And it was free. When the soiled moss was thrown away, it did not clog up the countryside as today's disposable diapers do; it disintegrated.

The children's job before the snow came and covered everything was to gather moss that was spread on a rack to dry. The rack was made by cutting a small spruce tree in half and turning the top half upside down. The dried moss was used for other things as well, including wiping up wet floors and for packing inside moccasins to keep the feet warm and dry against the icy winter.

According to the records of the Oblate Fathers, Father Lacombe had christened Victoria.[2] The date of her baptism is listed as the same day as her birth, which was a rare event at that time. Often a priest wasn't available to perform marriages or to baptize children until the child was a bit older.

In fact, according to the records, Victoria's father, Alexis Belcourt, was christened by Father Thibeault at the mission at Lac Ste. Anne on December 4, 1844, the same day his parents (Catherine L'Hirondelle and Joseph Belcourt) were married. He would have been 18 years old at the time, and four years later, on July 4, 1848, Alexis married Nancy.[3]

It was the common practice back then for couples to consider themselves married and even have a wedding celebration. When they were able to find a priest or visit one of the few far-flung missions, their union was made official. Marriage *à la façon de la payees* (in the custom of the country) was a common occurrence during the time of the fur trade. The marriage ceremony was a combination of Native and European customs.[4]

With the arrival of the missionaries, couples could make their union official, though many fur traders did not do this. They often left their Native and mixed-blood wives and children behind when they moved. But in 1861 in the Lac Ste. Anne area, this was not an issue. The couples may have been forced to wait to make their marriages official, but they were eventually married by a priest when it was possible to do so.

Twelve years after Alexis and Nancy were married, baby Victoria came along. Had Father Lacombe somehow been travelling nearby and dropped by the Belcourt cabin the day Victoria was born? It's much more likely that when her family visited the mission to have her baptized, the event of her birth and baptism were given the same date. It is possible that she was born earlier and that the date on the record was for her christening only, since no birth certificates were issued in those days, but we will never know. Regardless, her family always celebrated November 19 as her birthday.

She was named "Victoria" for the Queen, and "Anne" for the saint—Saint Anne would be her patron saint. Lac Ste. Anne was Victoria's home for most of her life, and she always believed that the waters of the lake were special.

Chapter Three

The World She Was Born Into

VICTORIA ANNE WAS BORN into a world that was untouched by the events going on outside the community. Canada would not become a country until she was nearly six years old. By the time Alberta became a province in 1905, she was 43 years old—and already a grandmother![1]

But even though the Métis families at Lac Ste. Anne might have been unaware of it, the world was changing. In the United States, 1861 was the year the Civil War began. In fact, Victoria was born on the day of the first battle in Oklahoma Territory (also known as "Indian Territory"). The battle of Round Mountain was an attempt by the Confederate Army to persuade the local tribes to join them in the war.[2]

Closer to home in southern Alberta, the whiskey traders coming north across the "Medicine Line" (as the border between the U.S. and Canada was known) to Fort Whoop Up (now Lethbridge) were causing death and destruction among the tribes of the Blackfoot Confederacy.[3]

Even the Métis families of Lac Ste. Anne in northern Alberta were aware that they must protect themselves from attack by enemies. Victoria recalled the time later in her life when her family went on a buffalo hunt. Even though hundreds of Red River carts and families travelled together, they still had to be careful. Once they were south of the North Saskatchewan River, "Riders would scout on ahead to see we did not run into our enemies. There were no police—no law."[4]

It would not be until 1874 when the newly formed North-West Mounted Police arrived in the area that the situation in southern Alberta improved. Around Fort Edmonton it was much more peaceful. The Hudson's Bay Company did not approve of trading for alcohol. In their more southerly forts, such as Rocky Mountain House, this rule often lost them valuable trade because the American whiskey traders sometimes set up camp outside the forts and competed for furs that were brought in for trade.

The voyageurs who settled near Lac Ste. Anne with their Native (usually Cree) wives were able to live in relative peace, hunting, trapping and trading at Fort Edmonton. Unlike the replica Fort Edmonton of today, the original fort was situated near the foot of the hill between the North Saskatchewan River and where the Legislature building now stands. When people arrived to trade at the fort, they pitched their tipis nearby.

Métis family ties were strong, not only because of the affection they felt for one another, but also because a solitary family would be unprotected in the lawless frontier. A strong support system meant that food from a lucky hunt was shared, and that other men and women were always close by to protect one another.

As well, the establishment of the missions at Lac Ste. Anne and St. Albert meant that someone other than the elders of the community was there to turn to should disputes get out of hand.[5]

Transportation back then was by horse or ox team, and Fort des Prairies was a day's journey from Lac Ste. Anne. Although the Belcourts were able to live off the land, which provided nearly everything they needed, they traded for a few extra items.

Often the men made the journey to the fort alone, but sometimes the whole family went. Victoria recalled that their tipi had been pitched on the bank where the Macdonald Hotel now stands.[6]

So baby Victoria and her family lived in an independent and self-sufficient community little influenced by the events going on in the outside world.

Chapter Four

Childhood and Family

SOON BABY VICTORIA WAS crawling around the cabin, keeping the whole family busy watching that she did not get too close to the open fire. Victoria was the baby in the family until she was nearly four years old, at which time her baby sister Athanese was born. Sadly, this little girl lived only five years. Nancy Belcourt used all her knowledge as a medicine woman, but despite her skills with herbs and tender care of the family, little Athanese died.

Until the little girl's tragic death, the Belcourts had been lucky to have strong, healthy children. In those days, few families had not buried a child or two. No hospitals or doctors were available, and no antibiotics existed to treat infections. If an illness could not be cured by using herbal pastes and other remedies, children died.

Victoria was nine when she lost her sister Athanese. Even though she also had her baby sister Virginie, who was three when Athanese died, a three-year-old was not as much fun as a five-year-old to play with. Victoria missed her little sister.

Although the cabin seemed somehow emptier without Athanese, it was hard to be lonely with so much going on. Work always had to be done. Families in those days were like small businesses, and even the smallest-sized "employees" contributed to keeping the company running.

At the age of nine Victoria was the chief baby-sitter and playmate for little sister Virginie. It wasn't hard work, but it kept her busy. She welcomed the time when she managed to get the little girl to take a nap on the pile of buffalo robes and Hudson's Bay blankets stored along the walls of the cabin.

When Victoria was 10, another baby Belcourt arrived, and they named him Joseph. Alexander, the only boy of the family, had wished for a brother, but Joseph's arrival came too late for Alexander to enjoy his new sibling. By that time, Alexander was 19 and already working away from home. Baby Joseph had to make do with sisters as playmates until he was four, at which time another boy baby arrived.

When John was born, Victoria was 14, a busy, hardworking girl. One more baby joined the family in 1882, Mary Jane Euphasine.

Not only did Victoria help her mother with the younger children, but she also learned to cook and prepare hides for moccasins and clothes. Soon she became an expert at the decorative beadwork that Métis women were famous for. Although originally the women of the Plains tribes used dyed porcupine quills to decorate their family's clothes and saddles, Métis women used small glass beads they could trade for at the local trading posts.

The fur trade companies brought in beads that were made of glass and manufactured in Italy or Bohemia. The beads were strung together in loops or small skeins and sold either by the string or by weight.

These tiny beads, known as "seed beads," were used as decoration on leather clothing. Instead of using fine jeweller's needles to work them, the women found that sinew could be stretched thin to accommodate the beads, and the end of the sinew was hard enough to thread the beads directly onto it. A regular needle could then be used to poke holes in the leather. Larger beads, sometimes known as "pony beads," were sold by the pound and used for necklaces or for decorating saddles.[1]

Métis women did not use the geometric designs of the Plains tribes but developed their own patterns. Some believe that these floral patterns were based on the embroidery patterns learned from the French nuns in the Red River area in Manitoba. Others think the patterns were inspired by the prairie flowers, particularly the distinctive wild prairie roses. Because of the type of patterns they used, the Métis were sometimes referred to as "The Flower Beadwork People."[2]

A beaded vest made by Victoria Callihoo

A beaded bag made by Victoria Callihoo

The Belcourts purchased very few items at the fort. Nearly every household item was handmade. The women made a coffee-like drink by cooking barley in a frying pan until it was nearly black. Then Nancy Belcourt or one of the girls boiled it and strained out the barley before serving the drink. Even though it was strong and black, it didn't taste much like coffee!

Barley was used in soup, too. To prepare it, the women soaked the barley in lukewarm water, drained it and then poured the softened barley into a hole bored 6 to 8 inches deep and 7 inches across in a block of black poplar (30 x 16 inches). A home-made block of wood that fit into the hole was then used to pound the barley to remove the hulls. It took a while to sort the hulls from the barley, and so this was a job usually given to the younger children. The final softened, cleaned grain could then be added to the soup.

The Métis people made soap for washing as well. They used the grease or fat leftover from cooking and mixed it with ashes and lye. Called *la potash*, it was certainly not as gentle as some of the soaps we use today, but it produced a good lather and got things nice and clean.

Brooms were homemade, too, using the slender branches of willow tops. These were tapered to a fine end and cut in two-foot lengths. A large stick about four feet long was selected for the broom handle. Then about a hundred of the finely tapered tops were bound around the handle. It worked!

Twig brooms made by Victoria Callihoo

Once the broom was constructed, Victoria could now do another of her jobs—keeping the floors swept clean.[3]

The women of the household also spent much of the day preparing food. Stew or soup was usually found simmering in a pot that hung in the mud fireplace. The youngsters often snared rabbits for the soup pot, but an abundance of other game was also available. Ducks, geese, partridge and grouse were staples. The men also hunted moose, deer and occasionally bear. Bear meat was a delicious treat and tasted like pork, especially if shot in the fall before the animals lost their fat. The Belcourts always shared any extra meat with relatives and other families in the settlement.

Thanks to the lake, the people in Lac Ste. Anne had more variety than Métis families in other areas who lived solely on game that was trapped or hunted. The lake provided plenty of whitefish, and fishing was an important activity for the men. The fish could be roasted, fried or boiled. And some of it was smoked and stored for use later.

The fish also provided extra trading power for the family at the fort. The community of Lac Ste. Anne provided thousands of fish each year to Fort Edmonton. According to the records for one year in the early 1860s, 10,000 whitefish were traded at the fort, which was 20,000 fewer fish than they normally took from the lake.[4]

When the family gathered together for a meal, everyone sat on the floor to eat. Meals were served on a canvas cloth spread over a tanned hide so that the food didn't touch the dirt floor. The family sat on the hides and blankets that were folded and placed along the edge of the room.

"We had no tables, no chairs or benches," Victoria later recalled, and "because we didn't have them, we didn't miss them."[5] The lack of furniture was probably a good thing, too. Imagine having a one-room cabin with a dozen people living in it—there wouldn't be room for furniture!

The Belcourts always had plenty of good food to eat, thanks to the good hunting and fishing skills of the men and boys, and the good cooking of the women and girls of the family.

Chapter Five

Springtime Activities

Spring was the best time of year. The children enjoyed being free from the heavy winter clothing. And by the time winter released its freezing grip on the little settlement at Lac Ste. Anne, everyone was tired of the long, dark winter.

Once the days got longer, the young ones couldn't be kept indoors. Moccasins were made for running, leaping puddles and finding the dry places between the stubborn patches of snow that still resisted the sun. It was as if a group of prisoners had been released.

In the spring, Victoria helped to plant the garden. Potatoes and other root vegetables were planted first because they were hardy plants that would not be hurt by the late-spring frosts. Cabbages were also planted because they could be easily stored for the winter. These were planted later, after the first full moon in June when all danger of frost had passed. The work of planting the garden was hard, but Victoria was strong, and happy to be out in the sun.

Planting potatoes was a family effort, at least for the children. One of the older children or Nancy had the job of cutting up the old potatoes that had been kept for seed or had not been used up over the winter. Each potato was cut into pieces, with at least one eye left on each piece so that the potato would sprout and grow a new plant. It was a time-consuming job because the potato patch took up a large part of the cultivated land. For the actual planting, someone either rode or led the horse that pulled the single-bladed plough while another child or two followed behind, dropping the cut-up potatoes into the rich soil of the furrow.

The family tried to grow more than they needed so that some of the potatoes could be sold to Fort Edmonton in the fall. In 1868, when Victoria was seven, records show that the little community at Lac Ste. Anne produced 700 barrels of potatoes, as well as 200 barrels of cabbage, carrots and onions.[1] These measurements only referred to what was provided for sale, so the crop was even bigger than that. The people had kept enough vegetables for their own use over the winter and some for seed purposes the following spring.

When the leaves on the poplar trees grew to the size of a squirrel's ear, it was time for the spring hunt. By this time the gardens and the small field of barley had been planted, and everyone could concentrate on preparing for the hunting trip.

The Red River carts had to be overhauled and made ready for the trip. Since the carts were made completely out of wood, replacement parts were easy to come by, but they had to be cut. No bolts, nails or screws were used to join the wooden pieces together, so large and small pegs had to be hand cut, and it took some time to make them. The harness for the horse or ox used to pull the cart was handmade from buffalo hide, and this too required a lot of work before the Belcourt family was ready to begin their journey to hunt buffalo.

Chapter Six

Buffalo Hunts

THE MEN OF THE COMMUNITY of Lac Ste. Anne met to organize and plan the buffalo hunt. A leader was chosen, and he and his "lieutenants" decided on the departure date. The hunts were organized with almost military precision, and strict rules were established to keep order among the hundreds of participants.

There were four main rules:
1. No buffalo were to be run on Sunday.

2. No group was to cut away, go ahead or lag behind.

3. No person or party was to run buffalo before the general order.

4. Every captain with his men must patrol the camp and keep guard.

Punishment for breaking the rules:

1. For the first offence against these laws, the guilty party would have his saddle and bridle cut up.

2. For a second offence, the shirt would be removed from the offender's back and cut up.

3. For the third offence, the guilty party would be flogged.

4. Any theft, no matter how small, was punished by having the offender brought into the centre of the camp and his or her name was called out three times, adding the word "thief" after each time.[1]

Humiliation in front of the community was considered the most severe punishment rather than loss of possessions or freedom. In a community as close-knit and dependent on each other as the Métis were at that time, public disapproval from their friends and families was a much more powerful deterrent. The Métis were a proud people, and losing face mattered much more to them than losing mere possessions.

For Victoria as a young girl, these regulations were probably something she didn't pay much attention to, though the rules did make the hunt run more smoothly.

Early on the morning of their departure for the hunt, the carts were loaded with tents and tipis. They took little in the way of food because the hunters hoped to find some game on the way. And once the hunt began, they feasted on the buffalo that were killed. But they did bring along tea and perhaps bannock to be eaten whenever they stopped. The Belcourt family took three carts on the buffalo hunt, but only the youngest child rode; everyone else walked because the carts moved so slowly. The usual speed was four to six kilometres per hour. There was no danger of the children falling behind at that speed![2]

Victoria's family and the rest of the people from Lac Ste. Anne were the first to set out on the buffalo hunt. Their carts followed the leader who had a flag flying from his cart to show he was in charge.

As they travelled south, other Métis settlers from St. Albert joined them. Sometimes more than 100 families travelled together. In total there might be almost 300 Red River carts jolting over the uneven ground. With no springs on the cart to ease the rough ride, it's easy to understand why everyone preferred to walk.

Some years, the groups that took part in the buffalo hunt were even larger if they travelled as far south as Tail Creek on the Red Deer River, where other hunters joined them. During the 1800s, Tail

Creek was the largest settlement between the Red River in Manitoba and the Rocky Mountains.[3]

Although not as large as some of the hunts from the Red River settlement, the hunts Victoria's family took part in each year were substantial. No records were kept of their actual hunts, but a Red River hunt in 1840 was recorded to have had 620 hunters, 650 women, 1210 Red River carts, 655 horses, 586 oxen and 542 hungry dogs! During that particular hunt, 1475 buffalo were killed and nearly one million pounds of pemmican were produced.[4]

A buffalo hunting trip was also an opportunity for people to get together and visit. Children played tag and ran about as they followed the long procession of carts. Sometimes Victoria and her sisters picked prairie flowers: crocuses or even a few early buffalo beans. For the children, going on the hunt was like a holiday.

In order to get to the plains where they would find the herds of buffalo, the people on the hunt had to ford rivers and streams. If they came upon a small stream, the people walking could wade across, but to cross deeper rivers, the wooden carts were floated across, while the horses and oxen swam to the other side. The North Saskatchewan River was the most difficult crossing as it was the deepest and could be dangerous. Traditionally, the best place to ford was a spot near where

Edmonton's High Level Bridge is today. Everyone was relieved once they crossed the river.

Reaching the river also meant that within a day's travel they would find the herds of buffalo that had moved northward to feast on the new spring grass of the prairie. In Victoria's day, the herds of buffalo were so huge that the plains were covered with a dark, moving mass.

Later in her life, Victoria dictated her memories of a hunt she went on in 1874 when she was 13: "We, of those days, never could believe the buffalo would ever be killed off, for there were thousands and thousands." It was impossible for anyone, especially a young girl, to imagine that her future children would never experience a hunt or see the vast herds of plains bison she had known. In the U.S., more than three and a half million buffalo were slaughtered between 1872 and 1874,[5] but the huge herds that Victoria saw were still feeding on the Canadian prairies at that time.

Once the young men had scouted out the herd, the families set up camp while the buffalo hunters rode out. They lined up, often several hundred hunters abreast a mile or two from where the herd was grazing. At the signal from the leader of the hunt, the men began to move slowly at first and then trotting, and then finally as they came closer, riding at full gallop. They rode with the sun at their backs so that their view of the herd was clear. It also gave them even more of an element of surprise over the peaceful herd.[6] The bulls might show defiance, but soon they panicked and, too late, began to stampede.[7]

Métis men were renowned for their horsemanship. They demonstrated their prowess during each hunt. Buffalo hunting was dangerous work. Racing over the uneven ground, a horse might step in a gopher hole or be gored by a wounded animal. The men rode among the stampeding animals, and often a rider was thrown and trampled. The greatest number of injuries that occurred were from falls.[8]

The horses used in the hunt were known as buffalo runners and were trained to do that job. The buffalo runner was not ridden on the trip to the hunt but was led along by its owner, who rode one of his less important horses. He wanted to save the buffalo runner's strength for the actual chase.[9]

The buffalo runners had to be intelligent, sure-footed and courageous. The horses had to be able to turn and change directions quickly at the rider's command. Only the owner of the buffalo runner was allowed to ride it. And like their riders, these horses had amazing stamina. Not many horses qualified for the job of buffalo runner, but the Métis were able to train them well. These horses raced alongside the herd of stampeding buffalo until their rider picked his target animal and shot it. If the herd was large, the rider might be able to kill several buffalo before the run was completed. Although the average number of buffalo killed per hunter might often be only three or four, Victoria told Grant MacEwan that Abraham Salois, a hunter from St. Albert and Tail Creek, was reported to have killed 37 buffalo on a single hunt.[10]

It was not the lack of target animals that dictated how many animals could be shot. The difficulty was in reloading the old muzzle guns that most of the men carried. Imagine riding at full speed and having to reload your rifle at the same time. Reloading was not a simple matter of fitting a shell into the chamber, either. The old flintlock muskets and muzzle loaders of the day required that the gunpowder and lead shot be shoved down into the barrel of the gun, a complicated operation even when standing on firm ground and using both hands. To reload his rifle, the hunter filled his mouth with the heavy balls, then spat them into the muzzle of the gun.[11]

Riders also carried powder horns and rags slung over their shoulders.[12] They had to pour the right amount of gunpowder down the barrel of the gun. Powder horns had a lid to measure, but riders had no time to do this while they were galloping alongside a herd of stampeding buffalo. The men knew instinctively how much gunpowder to add.

Then they followed the powder with a piece of greased cloth and some lead shot and used a ramrod to push it all down to the bottom of the barrel.

Finally, they had to cock the gun halfway to add a few more grains of gunpowder. When the gun was fully cocked and the trigger pulled, the hammer hit the flint, which threw a spark to ignite that last little bit of gunpowder. The small explosion set off the remaining gunpowder in the gun and sent the lead shot out of the barrel.

In order for the hunter to carry out this procedure successfully, his buffalo runner had to be sure-footed. A rider held the reins in his teeth and used both hands to reload. Not an easy task. Horses that could follow the herd smoothly without shying away were vital to a successful hunt. A good, clean kill required that the animal be hit just behind and below the front shoulder, immediately behind the foreleg.[13]

Many of the men rode bareback, while others used homemade saddles of buffalo hide that were then stuffed with buffalo hair or the long soft grass known as "prairie wool." The saddles might be decorated with beadwork on the corners that extended beyond where the rider sat. Stirrups were made from buffalo hide that was dried when "raw" (that is, not tanned or cured in any way, so that the leather was thick and hard).

Because the hunters had to ride so close to the stampeding herd, there was always the danger that a horse might stumble, or a rider could fall and be trampled. Broken bones were common, and it was in these situations that Victoria's mother's wisdom as a medicine woman was needed. Nancy set broken bones and prepared medicines from herbs to heal the many injuries fallen riders might suffer.

Although the greatest danger was falling from your horse during the stampede, after the herd had passed and the men dismounted, one of the fallen buffalo that had not been fatally wounded would often get up and attack anyone near it. If this occurred and one of the men was gored, his wounds had to be cleaned and treated with healing herbs.

Female buffalo were the most dangerous because they could turn and attack so quickly and unpredictably that frequently even the cleverest hunter was caught unawares. A bull might gore in passing, but he would then keep on going. A cow buffalo, on the other hand, would sometimes turn and continue to attack no matter how hard the hunter tried to avoid her. As well, the cows could run for hours with only the fleetest horses being able to keep up.[14]

Once the herd was at full run, the cows ended up leading. After the cows came the bulls, and at the back were the calves.[15]

"Nobody liked veal," Victoria recalled in later years.[16] And unless the calves were very young, they survived to live with the herd after the run was over. This meant full-grown buffalo would be available for the next year's hunt.

Chapter Seven

The Buffalo— One-Stop Shopping!

ONCE THE BUFFALO HUNT was over, the women and older children helped to slice the meat and take it into camp. Victoria helped out by making a smudge fire to keep flies away from the meat. The trick to making a smudge fire was to add enough green grass (leaves could be used if trees were nearby) to prevent the fire from flaring up and to keep the smoke rising.

The adults made drying racks by suspending a long pole between two tripods that had been pounded into the ground. The strips of meat were then draped over the pole to dry. As long as no flies were allowed on the meat, it would not spoil.

One of the jobs for the younger children was to gather "buffalo chips" that were added to the smudge fire to keep it going. Buffalo chips are really manure—buffalo droppings that had dried in the sun until they were as hard as wood.

Often, on the prairies where trees were scarce, buffalo chips were the only source of fuel for fires. But they burned well. You might call them one of the first renewable non-fossil fuels to be used by man! Some early accounts referred to them as the "prairie travellers' fuel." The French term for them sounds much more elegant. *Le bois de vache* translates literally as the "wood of the cow," which is accurate if not very elegant![1]

Whatever you wish to call it, the buffalo chips provided fuel that burned well and, according to studies done in 1983, had more heating power after 15 minutes than either spruce or poplar wood.[2]

Gathering lumps of manure might not seem like one of the nicest jobs, but remember that the sun had baked them and dried them, and they were truly as odourless as any other bits of wood found on the ground. So even the young children took part in the huge operation of collecting buffalo chips during the hunt.

People used to refer to the buffalo as "the one-stop shopping centre." Victoria and her family knew the buffalo provided most of their needs: "We ate the meat, we used its hide for robes, shelter for our lodges, footwear, clothes and bags."[3] And as we have just learned, the animals also provided an excellent source of fuel for fires. Nothing was wasted.

In using the buffalo so completely, the Métis people were only following the example of their Native ancestors. At one time the thick skin on the neck of a buffalo bull was cured over fires and used as warriors' shields. This thick skin was also used to make the stirrups on Métis saddles. Native people found many uses for buffalo bones; the broken bones were made into scraping tools, the long rib bones were used as sled runners, and sinew was used to make bowstrings.[4] Although in earlier times the bladder could be used as a bag to carry water, often the Métis children blew it up and used it as a tough football. The bison horns were made into drinking cups or holders for the hunters' gunpowder, and the tail was used as a makeshift fly swatter!

Once the meat was dried, it was made into pemmican. An uncured buffalo hide was hung from six poles forming a hollow centre area into which they tossed the strips of dried meat. Two men, working from either end, then pounded the dry meat until it was broken up into a powdery substance. Sun-dried Saskatoon berries were often mixed in, as well as grease that had been rendered from the buffalo fat.

Author Grant MacEwan quotes Victoria remembering the pemmican later in her life: "Ah, that pemmican," Mrs. Callihoo said wistfully. "We didn't go for calves because we did not like veal, but when that meat from the grown animals was dried and pounded and mixed with fat and Saskatoon berries, it was the best food anybody could have."[5]

They packed the pemmican in buffalo robes and sewed it with sinew all around. Melted tallow, made from the fat of the buffalo, was used to seal the seams. The hair on the outside of the robe kept the pemmican well insulated from any kind of weather, and it kept very well.

Victoria's father, Alexis Belcourt, needed another man to help him lift this batch of pemmican onto the cart because a robe full of pemmican was heavy. But it was important to prepare as much pemmican as they could, especially at the fall hunt. They needed to ensure they had enough nourishing food to eat during the long Alberta winter, especially if they were unable to obtain fresh meat.

Chapter Eight

Growing Up—Religion

AT THE TIME OF VICTORIA'S birth in 1861, the mission at Lac Ste. Anne had already been established for almost 20 years. The Iroquois voyageurs who had settled in the area had not clung to their tribal culture. But these men remained steadfast in the Roman Catholic faith they brought with them.[1] Religion played an important role in Métis life, although visits from the missionaries were few and far between in earlier times because of the vast distances between prairie settlements. Métis people took any opportunity to have children baptized or marriages performed even if they had to cross religious lines to do so.

In her book, *The Sun Traveller,* Elizabeth Macpherson notes that an earlier member of the Callihoo family, Helene Beauregard, was baptized by Robert

Rundle, a Methodist, in 1841 and again by an Oblate priest in 1842.[2]

In 1861, Father Albert Lacombe set up the mission at St. Albert that, aside from his missionary work around the province, took up most of his time. He worked with the Métis people in both St. Albert and Lac Ste. Anne. Father Lacombe contended it took all his effort to reform these "drinking, gambling, merry-making people."[3] He even formed a Temperance Society in 1853. According to Lord Southesk, who visited the mission at Lac Ste. Anne in August 1859, those who joined the society were given a "handsome medal."[4]

Although the Native people of the area had always come to the lake for its healing powers, it was not until 1889 that Father Lestanc organized

Typical family camp in the early days of the pilgrimage

the first pilgrimage. It was held during the week of July 26, which is the Feast Day of St. Anne.[5]

Commemorating the special day of the grandmother of Christ blended well into the beliefs of the tribes who gave grandmothers a respected place in their culture. Over the next few years, the pilgrims to the lake included Cree, Montagnais, Assiniboine, Chipewayans, Beaver, Sarcee and Blackfoot, as well as the many Métis people of Alberta.

From the beginning, the pilgrimage attracted hundreds of people. Many came from far away, travelling by horse and wagon. For days, the dirt roads and trails were covered with a steady stream of wagons. The people heading to the pilgrimage camped along the way, often taking as long as two months to make the round trip to the shrine and back to their homes.

First Communion for Métis youngsters at Lac Ste. Anne Mission

In 1918, Father Patrick Beaudry OMI, a Cree-Métis priest from St. Albert, persuaded the Grand Trunk Railway to schedule a special train to take pilgrims from Edmonton and another to transport people from St. Albert, Morinville and Legal. Each year, the trains carried more than 2000 pilgrims before that special service was discontinued in 1936.

During the 1950s and 1970s, thanks to easier modes of transportation and good roads, approximately 10,000 people attended the two-day event every year. They came from all over the prairie provinces, as well as from Montana and other parts of the United States.

In the 1980s, the pilgrimage was expanded to five days to accommodate the increasing number of people attending. The number of languages used in

The Lac Ste. Anne pilgrimage was an opportunity for Métis people to get together.

the sermons was also increased from the original Cree, French and English to include several other Aboriginal languages.

Victoria needed no persuasion to be an enthusiastic supporter of the pilgrimage—she had learned of the lake's healing properties from her mother. Victoria was a young woman of 27 years when the pilgrimage began, and she attended every year until she was nearly 98 years of age.

But the pilgrimage was not only a religious event. It also became a wonderful time of reunion for the far-flung Métis families from the area. In a way, it

By the 1930s, pilgrims came by wagon and automobile to Lac Ste. Anne.

replaced the buffalo hunt as an opportunity for Métis families to gather together.

Herb Belcourt, in his book *Walking in the Woods: A Métis Journey,* describes his own pleasure at attending the pilgrimage: "To me the Lac Ste. Anne pilgrimage is a reunion: for friendship, for storytelling, as you walk around the tents and motorhomes, I enjoy listening to the stories and the laughter."[6]

Doubtless many others would agree. The pilgrimage was and still is an important gathering for Métis and Native people. In 2004, the Lac Ste. Anne Shrine was designated a National Historic Site.[7]

As well as providing for the religious needs of the Métis families, the Oblate missionaries tried to provide education in the Lac Ste. Anne area. In 1859, three nuns of the order of the Sisters of Charity, called the Grey Nuns, opened a school at Lac Ste. Anne Mission, but they left soon after. Father Lacombe's own sister Christine came and taught for a short time, but she did not stay either.

Many of the children growing up at that time never had a chance to learn to read and write. Victoria was one of them. By the time a permanent school was established and teachers were supplied in 1879, Victoria was 18 years old, already a married woman with a daughter of her own.

Chapter Nine

Young Womanhood

THE TERM "TEENAGER" IS A relatively modern one. In Victoria's day, Métis girls went from being "children" to being young women by the age of 13.

Even young children had jobs around the home. Girls helped their mothers and cared for the little ones, and boys learned to hunt and fish with their fathers. By the time she was 12, Victoria was already able to cook and perform the many household tasks to keep the ever-growing family fed and clothed.

Remember that this was a time when very few items came from outside the settlement. Nearly everything was prepared at home, from food and clothing to ordinary household items. She might not have known how to read and write, but Victoria could prepare an animal hide, scraping away the hair, tanning it and sewing it into moccasins, skirts and shirts for her brothers and sisters. She also knew how to decorate these items with the intricate flower beadwork the Métis women were famous for.

As well as preparing the food and making clothing, Victoria learned to make soap, brooms, woven baskets and many other items needed in the family's daily life.

"We milked cows," she recalled. "We made our own milk-pans out of birch bark. We used the tiny long roots, which we got in the muskegs, to sew the pans and berry pots. We used heated spruce gum to close the seams and leaks of the birch bark pans."[1]

Although the work was hard, the Métis people worked for themselves in those days. No bosses told them when and where to do their jobs. Nature was their boss, so if one season the hunting was bad and not enough pemmican was made, or the winter was too severe and animals were scarce, they went without.

Much of the hunting and other work was done with members from the community, and they always found time to get together. Even building a cabin for a family was a community effort. The logs were hewn then placed flat side up to make a solid floor. The floor was rough; it was made of logs that had been cut in half using an eight-foot-long saw with a handle at each end. The one-storey homes were made of hewn spruce logs. In order to shape the logs, the men built a platform about 10 feet above the ground. A log was hoisted up to a man on top of the platform, and another man stood at the bottom. The top man pulled the saw up and then the other pulled down, sawing the log on the downward stroke.

When the cabin was completed, the owner invited everyone over to a dance to celebrate and thank all the helpers. The reputation for "merry-making" that Father Lacombe worried about was well earned, because the Métis knew how to enjoy each other's company when families got together. Some-one played the fiddle and soon the dancing began. By the time Victoria was a young woman, the Red River jig was well known by the Métis people of Alberta. Victoria learned to dance it well.

As the name of the jig suggests, this lively dance originated among the Métis of the Red River area in Manitoba. It had a mixture of origins. Some of the steps came from the French (*La Grande Gigue* of Québec), while other steps were adapted from Irish step dances, Scottish reels and the Highland fling. Other steps imitated the mating dances of prairie birds, possibly from the prairie First Nations people's prairie chicken dance. Whatever the origins of the steps, it soon evolved into a uniquely Métis dance.[2]

The fame of this Canadian dance spread, and the October 1860 issue of *Harper's Bazaar* described it as follows:

...fresh dancers taking the place of those on the floor every two or three moments. The men were stripped to shirt, trousers, belt and moccasins...and the women wore gowns which had no hoops...a black-eyed beauty in blue calico and a strapping Bois Brule, would jump up from the floor and outdo their predecessors in vigour and velocity—the lights and shadows chasing each other faster and faster over the rafters; the flame, too, swaying wildly hither and thither and above the thump of the dancers heels...the fiddle shrieks...[3]

The music that evolved to go with the dance is now sometimes referred to as "crooked music" because it is not always played at a four/four beat. Dancers must be quick and careful to keep time because the fiddler often changes the tempo.

Red River jig dancers do not lift their feet as high as those who dance the European jigs. It is said that when the jig is done well, it sounds like the galloping of horses' hooves.[4]

But life was not all jigs and dances or housework. The life of young Métis women was difficult. The "half-breeds," as they were called, were discriminated against in other the cities and towns where the population was predominantly white.

Luckily for Victoria, being a young Métis woman in Lac Ste. Anne did not carry any problems with discrimination. It was different for the daughters and wives of some of the fur traders. Many of the fur traders who had married and raised children with their "country wives" abandoned them and replaced them with wives from the groups of white women who came west.[5] Unlike the problems faced by some young women in the 1800s, the position of the Métis women in the Lac Ste. Anne area was secure. The community was self-sufficient, not only in their working lives but also in their personal relationships.

Today, young women can choose among many careers and professions. Fifty years ago their choices were limited, except in rare cases, to teaching, nursing or secretarial work. In Victoria's day, women had only one choice—wife and mother. It was what they were trained to do. And Victoria was no different.

Chapter Ten

Marriage—Background of the Callihoo Family

IT WAS ONLY A MATTER of time before Victoria caught the eye of young Louis Jerome Callihoo. They had grown up together, as their families had known each other for years, and Victoria was popular at parties when the "merry-making" Métis people got together. She had become an expert at dancing the Red River jig. Lively and laughing, she had her pick of the young men in the community.

Louis Jerome was named for his grandfather, an Iroquois voyageur like Victoria's own Belcourt grandfather. Louis' great grandfather on his mother's (Angelique Bruneau) side is thought to have travelled with the explorer David Thompson. Louis was born at Fort Edmonton, where his father worked, and Louis spent his childhood there. But then the Callihoo family moved to Lac Ste. Anne, where Louis spent his teen years. His father and his Uncle Michel ran a fishery there.

The tradition in Métis families at that time was for a young man and his father to visit the father of the woman the young man wished to marry. Once Louis and his father visited Victoria's father and asked for permission to marry, Victoria was asked whether she agreed with the arrangement. Her acceptance made the engagement final, and then the wedding was planned. No engagement period or engagement ring was necessary.[1]

Louis Jerome's friends rode out to invite everyone in the community to the wedding, which was the only announcement needed. By this time, the mission, which had been started in 1843, was well established so couples didn't have to wait for a priest to visit the community.

On the morning of January 2, 1879, one of Louis Jerome's best men drove 17-year-old Victoria to church in a horse-drawn sleigh decorated with ribbons. Another groomsman took Louis, who was 20, to the church. After the marriage ceremony, the new couple was welcomed by shotgun blasts into the air, and then everyone gathered for dinner (which was the noon meal at that time).

According to Dr. Anne Anderson in her book *The First Métis: A New Nation*, a standard menu was prepared for such an occasion, and Victoria and Louis

Lac Ste. Anne Mission Church 2009—taken on a January day like the day of Victoria's wedding in 1879

Jerome's wedding dinner was similar to the one below.[2]

The Menu

Meatballs as a specialty, fricassee style

Roast meats, hot or cold (never any turkey or chicken)

Potatoes, breads and bannock

Raisin pies

Apple pie made from dried apples

Rice and raisin puddings

Dried prunes

Tea

Once the meal was finished, the fiddlers began to play, and the people got up to dance. Reels (which are like modern square dances) and, of course, the Red River jig, were some of the dances they enjoyed, with everyone competing to see who could dance the best and for the longest time. Wedding festivities often continued for several days, so the popular young couple definitely had a wedding to remember with so many of their friends and family living close by.

Victoria and Louis Jerome settled down near her parents. And Victoria now had her own cabin to care for and meals to prepare for her husband and herself. She kept busy as always, tanning hides and doing the beadwork that was part of her Métis tradition. She and Louis Jerome had no trouble becoming part of the community since it was filled with their friends and relations.

On September 23, 1878, Louis Jerome's uncle, Michel Callihoo, signed Treaty 6 on behalf of his Cree band of Métis relatives and connections.[3]

Essentially, signing the treaty with the Canadian government meant the band members became status Indians under the Indian Act. They lost their right to vote and were required to build their homes on designated "reserve" lands. The Department of Indian Affairs administered and controlled the band's finances that were overseen by a local Indian agent.

The disadvantage of losing the right to vote must have seemed insignificant at that time when it is considered that the band obtained a large tract of fertile land free of charge. In addition to being given the right to hunt, trap and fish, the community had access to good stands of timber on the reserve. The band was aware that hunting and trapping would soon no longer provide a living and that it would be necessary to expand their farming activities. The treaty promised that the government would provide farm equipment and livestock. And a cash payment of five dollars per person was guaranteed, with the chief receiving $25 and the headmen $15 per year. Free medical care, education and relief in hard times were also guaranteed under the treaty.

The Michel Band, as it was known then, was given a reserve of 40 square miles (surveyed in 1880).[4] The land was located northwest of Edmonton on the Sturgeon River.

So it was that a group of Iroquois, French and Cree came to inhabit a so-called Cree reserve. It seems the government agents involved were not very strict at that time in deciding which people should be considered a band member! Originally, 48 families signed the treaty, including the Belcourt and Callihoo families.

Victoria and Louise Jerome moved to the Michel Reserve in 1880. By that time they had two children, Anne and Dio Leon.

The following year, tragedy struck Victoria's family. It was October 24 and, although the ice on the lake was still fairly thin, Victoria's parents had gone out onto the lake to do some ice fishing. The cracking ice gave them a warning, but they were unable to move away before their combined weight around the hole broke the ice. Both Alexis and Nancy fell into the freezing water.

Alexis managed to get a long pole across the hole for them to hold onto, but the ice kept cracking and breaking away. Thinking that Nancy's chances were better with only her weight on the pole, Alexis let go and tried to cling to the ice around the edges of the hole. At each attempt more ice broke away until his chilled fingers could no longer hold on. Finally, Alexis slipped into the icy water and drowned.

For two hours, Nancy held onto the pole in the freezing water before she was rescued.

Now a widow, Nancy Belcourt was left to raise her young family on her own. Luckily, Victoria's eldest brother Alexander was a young man in his twenties by then, but John was not yet 10, and Mary Jane Euphasine was just a toddler.

Although Victoria had two young children of her own, she and her married sisters were a great support to their mother at that time. Métis families were close, and children often visited back and forth. Cousins, nieces and nephews were more like sisters and brothers in the network of families on the reserve.

Life was still hard, though. They had to keep the large families fed and warm during the long winters, but they had plenty of fun and laughter, too. Loneliness was never a problem. The kettle was always on for tea when anyone came by. Hospitality was part of the Métis tradition handed down from the "kokums," the Cree grandmothers who had grown up in the close-knit tribal camps of their ancestors. Indeed, the Métis seemed to have perfected a way of life that was communal.

As was done in the buffalo hunts, large game was divided among the families, knowing that when someone else had good luck in the hunt for moose or deer, the meat would be shared as well. Sharing was not only a way of showing generosity, but it also guaranteed that no meat was wasted by spoiling, because these were the days before refrigeration.

However, finding wild game was often a problem. The buffalo were fast becoming extinct, and it was getting harder to find game close to the reserve. Louis Jerome and Victoria, like the other reserve families, tried to make up the difference by farming. They raised cattle, hogs, chickens and turkeys. Many of the Métis didn't like the taste of beef, preferring buffalo, but they were forced to adjust.

For a short while they tried to raise sheep, and Victoria spun the wool to make socks and mitts for her family. Unfortunately, raising sheep proved unprofitable as a couple of coyotes could destroy a flock of sheep in one night.

In addition to raising animals, the Callihoo family planted wheat, and after it was harvested they took it to the mill at St. Albert to make flour that would be baked into bannock. Barley and oats were grown to feed the livestock, and vegetable gardens were a mainstay of the family's food supply. They grew corn, pumpkins, cabbage, turnips and plenty of potatoes. The vegetables they grew were good, but the garden required a lot of work in planting, weeding and hoeing it all summer.

Trapping for the Hudson's Bay eventually took a toll on the wildlife. In 1867, 500 lynx pelts were traded at the HBC store in St. Albert. It was only a matter of time before income from trapping became scarce. Some of the men from the reserve bartered their labour at the mission in St. Albert. The men did repairs and hauled things from Edmonton in exchange for supplies, now that they had fewer furs to trade.

Chapter Eleven

Children

LIKE THEIR PARENTS BEFORE them, Victoria and Louis Jerome had a large family. By 1890, they had five boys and only two girls to help around the house: Anne, the eldest (11), Dio Leon (10), Lizzie (9), William (7), Adolphus (5), Vital Victor (2) and Henry (1).

That was the year Louis Jerome built his family a new house with glass windows to let in more light. The disadvantage for Victoria was that the busy mother had another job to do. Hide window coverings hadn't needed much cleaning!

Still, Victoria was grateful that the mud fireplace had been replaced with a cook stove. Enamelware replaced the old iron pots for cooking, though they were still used to make soap. Wallpaper now covered the log and mud-chinked walls, and homemade furniture was in their rooms. The families had to save a long time for luxuries, but as in every other Métis house, a crucifix hung on the wall, one of the first purchases Victoria made for her new home.

It was during this time that Victoria worked outside the home for a short while as cook for a survey outfit just north of St. Albert. She had to learn to make loaves of bread instead of the usual bannock. And she became famous for her delicious baked beans.

Another daughter was born to Victoria and Louis in 1895. She was christened Alvina but soon became known simply as Alice. Up until then, all of Victoria's babies had been healthy. But her good fortune didn't hold. Her daughter Caroline was born in January 1897 and lived less than one month. Another baby girl, Melvina, was born in December 1897. She lived into the new year but died in January 1898. Winters were hard enough, but even Victoria must have found January a particularly sad month. She had given birth to 10 children and lost two babies in a row.

In November 1898, John was born, and no baby was watched or treasured more carefully. The loss of her two baby girls had been hard on Victoria. Although infants often died in those days, the pain of losing a child never lessened.

Baby John was strong and healthy, but it was three years before Victoria gave birth to another child. Julia Mary "May" was born in 1901, and with the birth of another daughter, Bertha Victoire ("Vickie") in 1903, Victoria and Louis Jerome's family was complete. There were now 11 children in the family: Anne, Dio Leon, Hermine ("Lizzie"), William, Adolphus, Vital Victor, Henry, Alvina ("Alice"), John, Julia Mary and Bertha Victoire.

A family of 11 children might seem huge today, but for Métis families in those days, it was average. Indeed, in earlier times, families were even larger. Louis Jerome's Uncle Michel had 10 children with his first wife, and after her death, he remarried and had another 12![1]

Chapter Twelve

Educating the Children and Other Changes

NEITHER VICTORIA NOR LOUIS JEROME had the opportunity to learn to read and write as children, but they were determined that their own children would have an education. It meant the children had to go away to boarding school. The Order of Oblates of Mary Immaculate ran St. Joseph's Industrial School in High River, known as the Dunbow Industrial School. It was established by Father Lacombe and was the first agricultural school established for children of the Plains nations.[1] However, few of the local tribes people wanted to send their children to the school. Children who lived in the area and were sent to the school frequently ran away, so Father Lacombe decided he would encourage Cree families from near St. Albert to send their youngsters to the school. Sixteen children from the St. Albert area went to southern Alberta to attend. Most of them were from the Michel band, but several came from the Enoch and Papaschase bands near Edmonton.[2] The children from these bands were not so likely to run away. It would have been a difficult journey for them to get all the way home to Lac Ste. Anne.

High River is south of Calgary, and it was a long trip to take the children to school. In those days before automobiles, the journey had to be made by horse and wagon. But the Callihoo parents considered it worthwhile. The girls didn't have to go as far away as their brothers to get an education. According to daughter Vickie (Bertha Victoire), all of them attended the Grey Nuns convent in St. Albert.

The training the boys received was practical in nature. They learned mechanics and how to operate steam engines. They learned carpentry skills and shoemaking as well as fieldwork. The girls, aside from performing housework, were taught knitting and embroidery.

Being such a long way from home meant that there were no monthly trips home or even visits at Christmas and Easter, so it was not surprising that Victoria missed her two eldest children, Anne and Dio. Anne, in particular, would have been a big help to her mother at home.

Anne and Dio were the first to attend school in November 1885, but when Victoria and Louis

Jerome visited them the following August, they took the two children home with them.[3] Dio returned to the school by February 1889, though Anne did not accompany him. No doubt she was learning all the necessary homemaker's crafts at home with her mother.

The school records kept by the Oblates described Dio as being "intelligent and a good worker."[4] He graduated in blacksmithing and farming. William earned a Level Four in farming. Adolphus and John didn't do as well as Vital Victor and Henry who achieved Level Five. Nevertheless, all of the boys did well.

Father Lacombe's plan of having children from the Lac Ste. Anne Michel Reserve attend school was a good one. In the 1880s, the Callihoos represented nearly one-third of the student population at the Dunbow School.

St. Joseph's Industrial School, High River (1888). At least eight of these children are Callihoos.

A few of the children from the local Peigan band must also have attended because William eventually married a Peigan girl named Anne English, whom he had met at the school.

Some of the knowledge about farming and machinery that the boys acquired was put to good use by their father. Louis Jerome had bought a steam threshing outfit, but until Vital Victor graduated, he didn't have anyone who could operate it.

Louis Jerome took advantage of all the spruce and white poplar that grew near their home and bought a sawmill. He was able to provide his own lumber for improving the buildings around the farm as well as bartering and selling to neighbours on the reserve.

But the sawmill proved to be an unhappy addition to the family. In 1915, 17-year-old John, home from school, caught his pocket in the machinery and was pulled into the blade. His horrible death broke Victoria's heart. She could no longer stand the machinery that reminded her of the tragedy. She insisted that they sell the sawmill and move away from their home on the reserve. They bought some farmland in nearby Lac Ste. Anne and built a new home.

The house was a far cry from the old log cabin where they'd started their married life; it was a fine two-storey home painted white with blue trim.

They also had an icehouse. Blocks of ice were cut from the lake in winter and placed in the cellar of this building. Covered over with sawdust for insulation and protected from the summer sun by the building, the cellar was the old-fashioned version of a refrigerator. Milk and other perishable food could be kept there. Victoria also had a milk house where she separated the cream from the milk she got from their small herd of cows. She also churned butter and sold it.

In her new community, just as she had been on the reserve, Victoria was in demand because of her knowledge of using healing herbs and wild plants. Her Cree mother had taught her these skills, and Victoria was often called to the bedside of the sick or dying.

In those days doctors were still unheard of in that part of the province, even if the people could afford to pay. Whether from her belief in the religious healing of St. Anne or from her mother's Native beliefs, Victoria always believed strongly in the ability of the waters of Lac Ste. Anne to cure minor medical problems.

Next to their farm stood a hotel, which Louis had purchased without telling Victoria of his plan. Whether he did this as a special surprise or was concerned that she might not be thrilled with the prospect of running a hotel and the attached coffee shop is not known. Whatever the case, she ran both establishments well. The hotel was a popular stopping place for travellers going to the mountains. They could spend the night and allow their horses to rest. It was a "Temperance" hotel; in other words, no alcohol was allowed. Because of this rule, the hotel gained a reputation as a safe, quiet place to stay.

Although running the coffee shop kept Victoria busy, Louis Jerome was pleased that it also provided a good place for his daughters to work. Soon the coffee shop was a popular meeting place. Victoria's friendly nature meant that laughter always went along with the good food.

By 1921, all the Callihoo children except Dio were married with homes of their own. Victoria and Louis Jerome moved back to the Michel Reserve and built another home there. By that time, the couple had 20 grandchildren, so Victoria still had a busy home life.

Chapter Thirteen

Wife of Chief of the Michel Band

MICHEL CALLIHOO (1824–1911) WAS Louis Jerome's uncle. He had been chief of the band that was named after him since the reserve (#132) had first been set up in 1878. After Michel's death, Louis Jerome was elected chief of the Michel band. Another phase of life for Louis Jerome and Victoria was about to begin.

By that time, many people had left the reserve. There had been problems with the regulations and interference of the various Indian agents. Often the band did not receive the material they had requested. If the band members went to the Indian agent in Stony Plain and requested ploughs and harrows, they were told none were available.

At one point, people on the Alexander Reserve killed a heifer when they were short of food, and

Agent de Caze cut their rations. Whether he did that to replace the cost of the heifer or as punishment isn't known, but such arbitrary actions by the Indian agents were common.

The Michel band had a similar problem in 1889 when, without the permission of Indian Affairs, they traded seven steers for a mowing machine, a rake and three wagons. The band members who had made the trade argued that they had raised the steers and therefore could trade them. The government argued that the steers were "presents" as defined in the Indian Act.[1] Such interference in the band members' attempts to improve their ability to farm must have been difficult for the independent Métis people to bear.

Regardless of the incident, the Michel Reserve was praised in reports to Indian Affairs: "…the homesteads compare very favourably with those of any White settlers. The houses are of a superior kind and well furnished. The stables and corrals are all substantial and well put up. Livestock is good and the Indians are well equipped with implements…. These Indians are industrious and law-abiding and far advanced in farming and civilization generally."[2]

Despite such praise, the disputes continued. In 1903, the band was taken to court because of money owed on purchases for equipment. Shortly after that the Michel band petitioned to be put on an "Independence List" so that they could manage their own affairs regarding sales of livestock and so on. The request was denied.

Given these circumstances, it is easy to understand why people began to leave the reserve. In 1890, only 95 people were recorded as living on the reserve, and in 1891 there were 37.[3]

The problems with Indian agents continued, and the Department of Indian Affairs pressured the band to sell off portions of their land. Of course, most of the profit from the sales went to Indian Affairs rather than to the band itself. According to the Indian Act, only 10 percent went to the band.

In 1906, the band wrote to Indian Affairs offering to quit the treaty in exchange for clear title to one section of land for each family. The request was refused.

It seemed that Louis Jerome became chief at a very unhappy time on the reserve. He remained in the position for only four years, and his cousin Solomon Callihoo (Michel's son) succeeded him in 1917.

Although many members of the band continued to live on the reserve, their numbers dwindled, until 1958 when the band members were "enfranchised" (given the right to vote) and lost their

Louis Jerome Callihoo (ca. 1898)

Indian status. "By 1962, all reserve lands and assets of the Michel Band had been distributed to its enfranchised members."[4]

In April 1998, the Indian Claims Commission of Canada recommended that a group known as the Friends of the Michel Society, representing the descendants and former members of the Michel band, be granted special standing to submit claims. "Approximately 660 individuals who are former members or descendants of the Michel band regained Indian status..." Their request for the band to be reinstated was denied. The Friends of the Michel Band now have the right to bring specific land claims.[5]

Chapter Fourteen

A Lifetime of Change

VICTORIA NURSED LOUIS JEROME WHEN he was dying of cancer. He died in 1926. For a while she stayed on the reserve, and then, in 1928, 10 Callihoo families, including Victoria's, decided to give up their Indian status and leave the reserve.[1] Victoria returned to Lac Ste. Anne and eventually moved to Gunn to live near her daughter Lizzie Vandalle. Victoria enjoyed many visits from her great-grandchildren, which at that time numbered 150![2]

Frieda Patterson of Onoway was a friend of Victoria's granddaughter Marie and remembers visiting as a 13-year-old. "There would be people over on Saturday nights...a party with dancing." And there would be Victoria, showing the youngsters how to do the Red River jig.[3]

Victoria Callihoo with buffalo robe—first prize in Red River jig competition

In 1935, when she was 74 years old, Victoria took part in a Red River jig competition in Edmonton. She beat out all the younger competitors to win the buffalo robe that was first prize.[4]

With a life that had spanned from a time of Red River carts to automobiles and from buffalo herds to shopping malls, Victoria managed to adapt to all the changes.

Grant MacEwan, in his book, *And Mighty Women Too*, states that at 90 years of age, Victoria's hair was still dark and "she had a nicely chiselled face showing fine character." She loved the old ways but adapted to the new. She had the first player piano in that part of the country and loved to sit and pedal, listening to the music as it played.[5]

Victoria neither smoked nor drank, and when she had the first medical examination of her life at the age of 99, it was no surprise to her when the doctor told her she was in excellent health.

Her recipe for a long, healthy life was: "Behave yourself and work hard!"[6]

Always regretting her own lack of education, she encouraged her children and was delighted when her grandchildren attended university. She preferred to speak a mixture of Cree and French, which is now known as the Michif language of the Métis people, although she was able to speak some English as well.

When she was 101 years old, Victoria spoke on the telephone for the first time. She was delighted to discover that she didn't have to speak English to use it. She was able to speak her own language and the instrument still worked!

In 1949, Victoria was invited to unveil the plaque at Elk Island Park commemorating efforts to save the prairie bison from extinction. How appropriate that a woman who had seen the last of the great herds and whose life had spanned the times when these great beasts were almost gone from the prairies should be there when the herds were saved.

There would never again be the hundreds of thousands of buffalo roaming free. As she herself described it, "We, of those days, never could believe the buffalo would ever be killed off, for there were thousands and thousands."[7]

Chapter Fifteen

Memories of "Queen Victoria"

LIKE THE QUEEN FOR WHOM SHE was named, Victoria became matriarch of a large family. At the time of her death in 1966 at the age of 104, Victoria Belcourt Callihoo had headed a clan of 11 children, 57 grandchildren, 165 great-grandchildren and 46 great-great-grandchildren and eight great-great-great-grandchildren.[1]

Stories about her life have become almost legendary. And among friends and family she was lovingly known as "Queen Victoria."[2]

Once when Victoria and her young son were walking in the woods, they came upon a bear. With typical courage she stayed with the bear "to keep an eye on him" while the boy was sent back to the cabin to get her old muzzle-loader. It didn't take him long to get back, and Victoria quickly killed the bear with one shot.[3]

Another story of her shooting ability didn't turn out as well. A hawk had swooped in among the chickens and was trying to fly away with her best rooster. Again Victoria got her gun, but this time she missed the hawk and killed the rooster.[4] The Callihoos feasted on chicken stew that day.

Victoria may not have had much schooling, but she was far ahead of most people when it came to "horse sense." A story is told of her wish to purchase a horse for driving when she was 90 years old. It seemed her grandson (Pat Callihoo) had one for sale and brought it to her so that she could have a look at it. He claimed the horse was seven years old. Victoria expertly opened the horse's mouth and looked at its teeth. "Pat," she said, "you can't fool your grandmother. That horse is twelve years old."[5]

Victoria lived alone in her home in Gunn until she was 101 years old. Each New Year's Day she held an open house for family and "anyone within driving distance."[6] Her usual farewell on these occasions was, "Now Happy New Year and I hope you'll be spared to be with me at the same time next year!"[7] Coming from a woman who was 100 years old at that time, this caused great amusement and only added to the affection everyone felt for someone with such determination and faith in her own survival.

Afterword

Finding Victoria

WHILE I WAS RESEARCHING THIS BOOK, I came across many sources that picked up the connection between John Rowand and Victoria Callihoo as being related. But I ran into trouble when I tried to check the details.

I began to compose a family tree for Victoria based on information at the Musée Héritage Museum in St. Albert. Thanks to my friend, the late Elizabeth Macpherson, author of *The Sun Traveller: A History of the Callihoos in Alberta*, there is a useful genealogy for many Métis families in the area. Truly an amazing project when you consider how difficult it is to obtain information about births, deaths and marriages in the days before government records were kept.

My family tree for Victoria looked like this:

John Rowand and Louise Umphreville

|

Antoine (Kinninawis?) Rowand m. Archange Nipissing

|

Nancy (Kinninawis) Rowand m. Alexis Belcourt

|

Victoria Anne Belcourt m. Louis Jerome Callihoo

Clearly, the family tree shows that Antoine Rowand, Victoria's grandfather, was the son of John Rowand and Louise Umphreville. With this information I began to follow the John Rowand line. It was there that I ran into trouble. The first clue to this was contacting my friend Janice MacDonald, author of *The Northwest Fort: Fort Edmonton*. Janice said there was a Nancy Rowand, daughter of the chief factor of Fort Edmonton, John Rowand, but Nancy had married James Harriot who was chief factor of the Rocky Mountain House Post.[1]

John Rowand and Louise Umphrieville had seven children (John Jr., Alexander, Henry, Marguerite, Sophia, Adelaide and Nancy), all very well documented in HBC records as well as in John's own journals. No Antoine is listed. Many things were said of John Rowand's character, but there was never any hint that he was unfaithful to his wife Louise.

In the early days, no missionaries existed to perform marriages. Instead, they were done "in the custom of the country" (*à la façon de la payees*), and the women were known as "country wives." Although John and Louise never officially wed, they maintained a relationship from 1810 until her death on July 27, 1849.[2]

Even when Sir George Simpson decreed that the traders should abandon the mixed-blood and Native women they had married *à la façon de pays*, John Rowand remained loyal to Louise.[3] Simpson himself had abandoned the Métis women he had lived with and who had borne him children.

In the Hudson's Bay Company Archives, John Rowand referred to Louise as "my old friend the Mother of all my children."[4] At her death, he notified his friends with the note, "the mother of all my children is no more."[5]

Was John Rowand's loyalty to Louise because she had rescued him from a painful death out on the prairie? The story has it that as a young clerk serving at the North West Company Fort Augustus, John Rowand had ridden away from the trading post. While hunting buffalo, he fell or was thrown from his horse. Seriously injured with a broken thigh bone, he could only lie there and hope by some miracle that someone would rescue him.

Although a search was organized when the riderless horse returned, only Louise had watched him leave and knew in what direction he had gone. So it was she who found him, managed to bind his leg and get him on her horse and back to the fort.[6]

Fred Stenson, in his award-winning novel, *The Trade*, suggests that Louise made Rowand promise to marry her before she would "rescue" him.[7] It's a possibility. The fact remains that the future chief factor of Fort Edmonton remained steadfast in that promise.

Louise is referred to in some early records as "a Cree woman living near the Fort," but she was only half Cree. When Louise was five years old, her father, Edward Umphreville, a trader in the Red Deer Hills, abandoned the family.[8] Louise and her brothers by Umphreville would have lived with her mother's people until they grew up. No doubt Louise was determined not to suffer the same treatment her mother had. Whether it was that determination or Rowand's promise, it seems we can be reassured that Louise was indeed the mother of all Rowand's children.

What of Antoine being a Rowand grandchild, making Victoria a great-great-grandchild of John Rowand? We can rule out the daughters, because for the Rowand name to be carried on, it would have to be through the sons. And for Nancy's brother to name his daughter after her aunt might seem reasonable.

However, considering the ages of Rowand's sons, a great-grandchild is not a possibility since the birth dates of John Jr., Alexander and Henry range between 1812 and 1820, and Antoine Kinninawis Rowand's date of birth (in the Musée Héritage Museum records) is given as (circa) 1809 at Lesser Slave Lake.

Even if there is an error in Antoine's date of birth, it does not seem possible for him to be the offspring of one of John Rowand's three sons. Henry died in 1835 at age 14 of "brain fever."[9] Alexander moved east at the age of 14 to attend school, and he lived in Montréal all his life, following in his grandfather's footsteps to become a doctor. There is no record of any of his children returning west. John Jr. became chief trader at Fort Pitt and married Margaret Harriot, the daughter from James Harriot's first marriage. (Chief Trader Harriot's second marriage was to Nancy Rowand, John Jr.'s younger sister.) John Jr. died on March 3, 1865, at his home near Fort Garry where he and Margaret had lived since 1856 when he left his employment with the Hudson's Bay Company.[10] Two children are mentioned in John Jr.'s will: a legitimate son, John James Alexander, and an illegitimate son, William Rowand.[11] John James Alexander died a year after his father, and there is no mention of his leaving any heirs.[12]

As I continued to try to make the Rowand connection fit into Victoria's genealogy, it seemed that at every turn the information did not fit. How could this connection have developed? The explanation lay in the Oblate Fathers' records, now located at the Provincial Archives in Edmonton. But a visit there only raised new issues. Although John Rowand was not Catholic, he was included in the records, which only added to the confusion.

Strangely, his first four children are listed as having been the offspring of "John Rowan et Adelaide." Who was Adelaide? Since John's activities after he joined the fur trade and came west are well documented—with no mention of a wife—could he have married before leaving Montréal? This is almost certainly impossible as he was 14 years of age and would not likely, given his social status (his father was a medical doctor in Montréal), be married at such a young age. Besides, the Oblate records indicate some of the children's birth dates: John in 1812, Alexandre and Adelaide in 1831, Marguerite (Peggy) in 1823, and Sophie in 1828. There is no mention of what became of the Adelaide who was supposed to be the mother of these children, but a later page indicates "John Rowand et Louise (Millet)

Umfrieville" and states they had two children: "Nancy (nee en 1808) and Antoine (nee en 1809)."[13]

At last the mysterious Antoine makes an appearance!

The entry for Antoine also includes the information, *"bapt. Le 14-9-42 au Ft. Edmonton et marie le meme jour a Archange Nipissing agee ou 25 ans, fille d'Ignace et d'une Saulteuse."* (Bapt. the 14-9-42 at Fort Edmonton and married the same day to Archange Nipissing aged 25 years, daughter of Ignace and a Saulteaux woman.)[14]

Of course, in those days, it was not unusual for people to be baptized and married at the same time since they might not have had the opportunity to do so at an earlier time.

Antoine has his own entry in the Oblate records as Antoine Rowand: *"Ne en 1809 de Sieur John Rowand et de Louise (Millet) Umphreville. Baptise le 14-9-42 par M. Jean-Bapt. Thibault a Fort Edmonton. Marie le 14-9-42 a Archange Nipissing (1817) fille d'Ignace et d'une Salteuse."* (Born in 1809 of Seigneur John Rowand and of Louise [Millet] Umphreville. Baptized the 14-9-42 by Father Jean-Baptiste Thibault at Fort Edmonton. Married 14-9-42 to Archange Nipissing [1817] daughter of Ignace and a Saulteaux woman.)[15]

There seemed to be difficulty in documenting events that occurred outside the priests' own experience, but there should be no doubt that the marriage of Victoria's maternal grandparents, Antoine and Archange Nipissing, can be accepted as fact.

Archange Nipissing came from a family that also had historic roots. In his book *Overland by the Yellowhead*, author J.G. MacGregor, when tracing the early Edmonton-Jasper route, mentions Father Lacombe making the trip in 1857 accompanied by his Métis guide Michel Nipissing.[16]

According to the Oblate records, Antoine and Archange had only two children. *"Annie ou Nancy (1830) bapt. le 14-9-1842, mariee a Alexis Bellecourt"* (Annie or Nancy [1830] baptized the 14-9-1842, married to Alexis Bellecourt), and *"Betsy (1839) b. 26-7-1842, mariee le 9-11-57 a Alexis Dumont, fils de Gabriel.* (Betsy [1839] b. 26-7-1842, married the 9-11-57 to Alexis Dumont, son of Gabriel.)[17]

Nancy, of course, was Victoria's mother. An interesting side note to this is that Victoria's Aunt Betsy married a son of Gabriel Dumont. This was not the Gabriel Dumont of Riel Rebellion fame but his uncle. According to George Woodcock's book, *Gabriel Dumont: The Métis Chief and His Lost World*, the older brother of Isadore (Gabriel's father) remained in Lac Ste. Anne when his two younger brothers moved to the Saskatchewan area.[18]

The elder Gabriel was considered one of the leaders in that region. This would mean that Victoria was related to one of western Canada's Métis heroes since her Aunt Betsy was young Gabriel Dumont's cousin by marriage.

Whether we can accept the parentage of Antoine as written is another matter. Did the Oblate priest recording John Rowand's family at a later date mistake his daughter for a wife?

There is evidence that the Oblates at Lac Ste. Anne did not always have a smooth relationship with the chief factor of Fort Edmonton. Father Emeric Drouin, in his book *Lac Ste. Anne Sakahigan*, mentions that Father Thibeault, founder of the mission at Lac Ste. Anne, "feels his style is cramped in Hudson's Bay forts where the Bourgeois are lords and masters, especially when it comes to John Rowand who, although a Catholic himself, is a very irascible autocrat more than one hundred percent dedicated to the interests of the Company. Woe to whoever crosses him or seems to imperil the self-claimed monopoly of the Honourable." The reference goes on to mention that "Even Fr. Lacombe will later have brushups with him."[19]

Although Father Lacombe may have had a few "brushups" with John Rowand, according to J.G. MacGregor's *Czar of the Prairies*, "he frequently expressed his love for John Rowand by saying, 'Ah! He was a grand little man.'"[20] It seems Father Thibeault did not share these sentiments, and it was he who kept the records for that period of time.

Could the whole John Rowand connection with Victoria have been an error?

A brief biography of Victoria Belcourt Callihoo as related by her daughter Vickie (Bertha Victoire) Kildaw and published in *The First Métis: A New Nation*, states that "Victoria Belcourt was born November 9, 1862 [sic], to Alexis and Nancy (Drouin) Belcourt."[21]

Suddenly a different name appears for Victoria's mother, Drouin. Could the name "Drouin" be mistaken for Rowand? A name that sounded similar might have been mistakenly put in the records. Once a mistake becomes family lore, it is sometimes repeated so often it is considered fact.

A new line of research opened up. There are no Drouins listed in the Oblate records. Indeed, the only Drouin I could locate was Father Emeric Drouin, author of the book previously quoted from *Lac Ste. Anne Sakahigan*.

Another dead end.

It is known that Louise Umphreville had at least one child before her country marriage to John

Rowand. A reference in George Linton's Slave Lake Journal in the winter of 1821 is quoted in *Czar of the Prairies:* "This evening three men came home with moose and hide shortly afterwards—Le Nipesangue, Mrs. Rowand's son and Campion arrived with their hunts…"[22]

This does seem strange. Are we to interpret this as meaning that "Le Nipesangue, Mrs. Rowand's son and Campion" are the three men who arrived with their moose and hides? Or were they followed by another three men?

The list is confusing, and at first glance, the reader might assume that "Le Nipesangue" referred to "Mrs. Rowand's son," and that only two men arrived shortly afterwards. It is unfortunate that he did not give "Mrs. Rowand's son" a name.

Did "Mrs. Rowand's son" use the Rowand surname? He must have been much older than his Rowand half-siblings since he was living as a hunter and trapper in Slave Lake while the eldest of them was only nine years old. It is feasible that "Mrs. Rowand's son" might have married the daughter or sister of his hunting companion. And Antoine, Victoria's grandfather, did marry Archange Nipissing (deviations in spelling often occur in early records).

Still, the Antoine Rowand mentioned in the records was born in 1809, and John Jr.—Louise and John Rowand's eldest son—was born in 1812, only a three-year difference. Could the Antoine Rowand I was trying to trace have been hunting in the Slave Lake area at the age of 12? It is possible—children grew up early in those days, but is it likely that Louise had a two- or three-year-old child when she and John began living together? There is no mention of this child in the Hudson's Bay records, nor in the journals or letters of those who visited the fort, although John and Louise's other children are frequently referred to.

The "Kinniawis" name is not traceable, either in the records of the Musée Héritage Museum nor in the Oblate records.

A clue finally emerged from Diane Lamoureux, who is in charge of the Oblate Archives at the Provincial Archives of Alberta. She told me that there were other Rowands in the Slave Lake area who were not related to John Rowand. Since Antoine was born near Lesser Slave Lake and not at Fort Edmonton as were all of John Rowand's other children, we may at last have solved the mystery.

That there were other Rowands seems much more likely than the possibility that two years before meeting John Rowand, Louise Umphreville was in Slave Lake giving birth to a child named Antoine and giving him the Rowand name.

So although Victoria might not be able to claim descent from that "irascible autocrat" John Rowand, "Czar of the Prairies," she still carried a wonderful Métis heritage, and because of her amazing life, deserves to be named our own early Albertan "Queen Victoria."

Endnotes

Chapter One

1. Simon, Steven. *Healing Waters.* Edmonton: University of Alberta Press, 1995, 7.

2. Strasbourg, Alvena (Laboucane). *Memories of a Métis Woman.* Edmonton: Self-published, 1997, 26.

3. Drouin, Emeric, OMI. *Lac Ste. Anne Sakahigan.* Edmonton: Editions L'Ermitage, 1973, 13.

4. Newman, Peter C. *Caesars of the Wilderness.* Canada: Viking/Penguin Books, 1987, 37.

5. Ibid., 38.

6. Cruise, David, and Allison Griffiths. *The Great Adventure.* Penguin Canada, 1998, 58.

7. Macpherson, Elizabeth. *The Sun Traveller: The Story of the Callihoos in Alberta*. St. Albert, AB: Musée Héritage Museum, 2003, 28.

8. Drouin, *Lac Ste. Anne Sakahigan*, 14.

9. Carnegie, James, The Earl of Southesk. *Saskatchewan and the Rocky Mountains: A Diary and Narrative of Travel, Sport and Adventure during a Journey through the Hudson's Bay Company Territories in 1859 and 1860*. Edmonton: Hurtig Publishing, 1969, 182.

10. MacDonald, Janice E. *The Northwest Fort: Fort Edmonton*. Edmonton: Lone Pine Publishing, 1983, 64.

11. Nicks, Trudy. "Missions Impossible," taken from: http://archiver.rootsweb.ancestry.com/th/read/METISGEN/2002-03/1015532508

Chapter Two

1. Author's memories of her own trapline as a child.

2. Oblates of Mary Immaculate, Records of the Order. xiv Registres de baptemes, Mariages et Sepultres Fort des Prairies. 1842–1888. 71.220/5213-5217. Provincial Archives of Alberta.

3. Ibid.

4. Van Kirk, Sylvia. *Many Tender Ties: Women in the Fur Trade Society.* University of Oklahoma Press, 1980, 4.

Chapter Three

1. Descendant Report, Métis Genealogy, Musée Héritage Museum, St. Albert.

2. Cooper, Wayne. "The Battle of Round Mountain—November 19, 1861," Art of the Oklahoma State Capitol. www.ok.gov/~arts/capitolart/permart/paintings/wcooper/roundmountain.html

3. Cruise and Griffiths, *The Great Adventure,* 103.

4. Callihoo, Victoria. "Our Buffalo Hunts." *Alberta Historical Review.* Vol. 8, No. 1, 1960, 24.

5. Foster, J.E. "End of the Plains Buffalo." *Buffalo.* Vol. 3, No. 1, 1992, 67.

6. MacEwan, Grant. "Victoria Callihoo: Granny." *And Mighty Women Too: Stories of Western Canadian Pioneers.* Saskatoon: Prairie Books, 1975, 195.

Chapter Four

1. MacDonald, *The Northwest Fort,* 63.

2. Racette, Sherry Farrell. *The Flower Beadwork People.* Saskatoon: Gabriel Dumont Institute, 1991, 12.

3. Callihoo, Victoria. "Early Life in Lac Ste. Anne and St. Albert in the 1870s." *Alberta Historical Review,* Vol. 1, No. 3, 1953, 23–24.

4. Macpherson, *The Sun Traveller,* 38.

5. Lac Ste. Anne Historical Society. *West of the Fifth.* [Local History]. Edmonton: Institute of Applied Art, 1959, 22.

Chapter Five

1. Macpherson, *The Sun Traveller,* 29.

Chapter Six

1. Chodin, Tim, and Dan Asfar. *Gabriel Dumont: War Leader of the Métis.* Edmonton: Folklore Publishing, 2003, 35.

2. Stories told to the author by her grandmother, Sarah Shearer, Saskatchewan, circa 1945.

3. Taylor, Cora. "Buffalo Hunters of Tail Creek." *Celebrating Alberta: Many Places.* Don Mills, ON: Pearson Education Canada, 2007, 12.

4. MacEwan, "Victoria Callihoo: Granny," 192–93.

5. Cruise and Griffiths, *The Great Adventure,* 101.

6. Newman, *Caesars of the Wilderness,* 161.

7. Verbicky-Todd, *Buffalo Hunting,* 147.

8. Ibid., 145.

9. Ibid.

10. MacEwan, "Victoria Callihoo: Granny," 192–93.

11. Verbicky-Todd, *Buffalo Hunting*, 149.

12. Callihoo, "Our Buffalo Hunts," 25.

13. Verbicky-Todd, *Buffalo Hunting*, 143–44.

14. Tellenius, Clarence. "An Artist Among the Buffalo." *Buffalo.* Vol. 3, No. 1, 1992, 133–44.

15. Verbicky-Todd, *Buffalo Hunting*, 143.

16. Callihoo, "Our Buffalo Hunts," 25.

Chapter Seven

1. Wright, Milt. "This Chip's for You Too." *Buffalo.* Vol. 3, No. 1, 1992, 229.

2. Ibid., 238.

3. Callihoo, "Our Buffalo Hunts," 25.

4. Newman, *Caesars of the Wilderness*, 159.

5. MacEwan, "Victoria Callihoo: Granny," 194.

Chapter Eight

1. Nicks, "Missions Impossible."

2. Macpherson, *The Sun Traveller*, 42.

3. Ibid.

4. Carnegie, The Earl of Southesk, 167.

5. Drouin, *Lac Ste. Anne Sakahigan*, 53.

6. Belcourt, *Walking in the Woods*, 28.

7. Lac Ste. Anne Pilgrimage website: http://www.lsap.ca

Chapter Nine

1. Lac Ste. Anne Historical Society, 23.

2. Métis Nation—Heritage Canada: www.metis-nation.ca

3. *Harper's Bazaar* excerpt, October 1860. Taken from Manitoba Historical Society: http://www.mhs.mb.ca/docs/pageant/07/redriverjig.shtml

4. "Interview with Yvonne [Chartrand] of Vnidansi" Louis Riel Day 2008. http://www.vnidansi.ca

5. Van Kirk, *Many Tender Ties*, 165.

Chapter Ten

1. Anderson, Anne. *The First Métis: A New Nation*. Edmonton: Uvisco Press, 1985, 319.

2. Ibid.

3. Macpherson, *The Sun Traveller*, 33.

4. Indian Claims Commission Report, 01/03/1998. http://www.indianclaims.ca/media/news-en.asp?id=232&content_type=2

5. Lac Ste. Anne Historical Society, 22.

Chapter Eleven

1. RootsWeb: METISGEN—Calliou/Callihoo—
History of St. Albert
http://archiver.rootsweb.ancestry.com/th/read/
METISGEN

Chapter Twelve

1. Macpherson, *The Sun Traveller,* 72.

2. Ibid.

3. Ibid., 83

4. Ibid.

Chapter Thirteen

1. Macpherson, *The Sun Traveller,* 65.

2. Ibid., 67.

3. Ibid., 65.

4. Indian Claims Commission Report, 04/03/1998.

5. Ibid.

Chapter Fourteen

1. Macpherson, *The Sun Traveller,* 75.

2. Ibid., 84.

3. Patterson, Frieda. Telephone conversation with
the author January 10, 2009.

4. Buffalo Spirit On-line, Victoria Belcourt Callihoo. http://www.ammsa.com/buffalospirit/2004/ footprints-VBCallihoo.html

5. MacEwan, "Victoria Callihoo: Granny," 197.

6. Ibid., 198.

7. Callihoo, "Our Buffalo Hunts," 25.

Chapter Fifteen

1. "Centenarian Dies in St. Albert Home." *Edmonton Journal*, April 22, 1966.

2. Lund, Carrielynn. Communication with the author October 10, 2007.

3. MacEwan, "Victoria Callihoo: Granny," 196.

4. Ibid.

5. Ibid., 197.

6. Ibid.

7. Ibid., 191.

Afterword

1. MacDonald, Janice. Communication with the author February 2007.

2. MacGregor, *John Rowand*, 154.

3. Van Kirk, *Many Tender Ties*, 207.

4. Ibid., 158.

5. MacGregor, *John Rowand*, 155.

6. Ibid., 20.

7. Stenson, Fred. *The Trade*. Vancouver: Douglas & McIntyre, 2000.

8. MacGregor, *John Rowand*, 20.

9. MacDonald, *The Northwest Fort*.

10. MacGregor, *John Rowand*, 174.

11. Ibid., 175.

12. Ibid.

13. Oblates of Mary Immaculate.

14. Ibid.

15. Ibid.

16. MacGregor, J.G. *Overland by the Yellowhead*. Saskatoon: Prairie Books, 1974, 72.

17. Oblates of Mary Immaculate.

18. Woodcock, George. *Gabriel Dumont: The Métis Chief and His Lost World*. Edmonton: Hurtig Publishers, 1975, 24.

19. Drouin, *Lac Ste. Anne Sakahigan*, 13.

20. MacGregor, *John Rowand*, 170.

21. Anderson, *The First Métis*, 144.

22. MacGregor, *John Rowand*, 62.

Appendices

Appendix I—Pemmican

LATER IN HER LIFE, VICTORIA CALLIHOO told Grant MacEwan, "it was the best and most nourishing food I ever ate!"[1] There is no doubt pemmican was an important staple in the Métis diet in her youth. Pemmican was eaten either raw, sliced, coated with flour and fried or cut up and made into in a thick soup called rababoo.[2] Adapted from the tribes of the plains, pemmican was a clever way of preserving food in the days before refrigeration or canning meat.

For early Native people, it was a food item that could be conveniently transported as they moved from place to place never knowing whether they would find game. They could carry pemmican with them or bury it to provide food later on. Properly prepared, it lasted months or even years. This staple was valuable indeed for people who might have difficulty finding game during the long prairie winters. Even today with the assistance of radio-transmitters attached to the animals and wildlife experts monitoring their movement from aircraft, wildlife migrations are difficult to predict. For early hunters who depended on game for their food supply, it was usually feast or famine. Pemmican saved lives.

Early explorers and fur traders coming on the long canoe trips into western Canada soon learned the value of an easily transported, reliable food supply. In time, the trading posts dealt not just in furs but in pemmican, prepared by the Native women who married voyageurs and settled near the forts. While the men trapped and traded in furs, the women's contribution was just as important. The voyageurs needed tons of this vital food to keep the supply lines of the fur trade in operation.

Victoria's memories of the taste of pemmican may have been coloured by the healthy appetite of a young girl, but some early traders showed less enthusiasm. In Peter C. Newman's book, *Caesars of the Wilderness*, H.M. Robinson states that one taster suggests that to imitate the taste of pemmican, one should, "Take the scraping from the driest outside corner of a very stale piece of cold roast beef, add to it lumps of rancid fat, then garnish all with long human hairs and short hairs of dogs and oxen and you have a fair imitation of common pemmican."[3]

Victoria's endorsement of pemmican as "the best food I ever ate" covered a great variety of food during her life. In the hundred years of her experience, beginning in her childhood in the late 1860s, she would have partaken of all kinds of food, all the way from pemmican to the fast food of modern times. That would give pemmican a lot of competition for "best food."

Victoria's radical difference of opinion might be explained by suggesting that Robinson's taster had eaten a bad batch of pemmican! If it was as loathsome as suggested in the quote, it's doubtful that the fur traders and early travellers would have adopted it with such enthusiasm to the extent that The Company of Adventurers Trading into the Hudson Bay (this was the original name of the Hudson's Bay Co.) would have continued to purchase (by trading) six or seven tons every year.

Opinions of the taste of pemmican varied. Henri Julien, an illustrator with the *Canadian Illustrated News* in Montréal, travelled with the newly formed North West Mounted Police on the march west in 1873 and reported in his diary, "We had pemmican for the first time and found it very good."[4] He wasn't alone. When a load of pemmican was brought to the camp, the men agreed it was "first rate stuff," and they quickly devoured the entire wagon full![5] Admittedly, the enlisted men had been existing on a diet of mainly biscuits and tea and so might not have been too critical. But Julien and the officers were enjoying better meals and more variety so their opinion of the taste of pemmican wasn't tempered by hunger.

The treatment of the meat used in making pemmican was fairly consistent. When the buffalo was butchered, the women cut the meat into strips and hung them on racks over the fire to dry. The fires aided in the drying process and kept the flies away.

Early Native woman making pemmican

Once the meat was thoroughly dried, it was pounded until it was a mound of powdery flecks. Although many references claim that this was a job for the women, Victoria recalls that men did this hard work. She describes a buffalo hide being suspended between six posts to form a U-shape. They threw in the dried strips of meat, and "two men on either end would then pound the dry meat into a pulp. Then sun-dried saskatoons would be mixed and grease would be poured in to make an even mixture."[6]

Recipes for pemmican vary. In his book on the fur trade, Peter C. Newman states, "The ingredients for a ninety pound bag of pemmican were simple: one buffalo to sixteen pounds of berries."[7]

The berries may have originally been added to improve the taste of the pemmican, but it was a brilliant move. The vitamin C in the berries was a vital source in preventing scurvy that might otherwise have followed a diet limited to meat. More than that, recent studies indicate that the tannins or tannic acid in the berries added a preservative that kept the bags of pemmican from spoiling. Tannins are astringent chemical compounds that are the plant's natural defence against fungal and bacterial attacks.[8] Although the berries did improve the taste, early pemmican makers may also have noticed that pemmican made with berries lasted longer.

"Pemmican" comes from a Cree word (*pimîhkân*) meaning "manufactured grease,"[9] and it may be that the variety of taste was a result not of the quality of the meat or the berries but from the fat that was added to the mix. The crucial ingredient in pemmican was neither the pulverized buffalo meat nor the dried berries but the animal fat. A diet of nothing but meat and berries would eventually be fatal.[10] The addition of buffalo fat to the mixture meant survival.

Early pemmican makers were aware that there were two kinds of fat found on the animal: hard and soft. The "hard" fat, or suet, is found deep in the body of the animal, around the organs. "Soft" fat is on the legs and just under the skin of the animal and includes the fat boiled out of the bone marrow. David Thompson wrote that he preferred the soft fat prepared in this way, "when carefully melted [it] resembles butter in softness and sweetness."[11]

The type of fat used in the preparation of pemmican depended on what was available on the animals they hunted. On a big hunt, such as the ones that Métis families like Victoria's took part in, there were ample amounts of the best fat, with plenty of the nourishing bone marrow included.

Once the pounded meat, berries and melted fat was thoroughly mixed, it was packed tightly in buffalo hides (with the hair on the outside) and, once all the air had been forced out, the hide was sewn tightly shut with sinew. The seams were then greased with tallow to make them even more airtight. Victoria remembers that these hide bags were so heavy it "usually took two men to load one on a cart."[12]

Because the fur traders required that the pemmican bags be the same weight as their bales of furs and trade goods, any bales the Métis prepared for trade probably weighed at least 90 pounds.

David Thompson praised not only the contents of these pemmican bags but also their packaging. They were, he wrote, "about thirty inches in length by near twenty inches in breadth and about four in thickness, which made them flat, the best shape for stowage and carriage."[13]

Any doubts about pemmican being the "best and most nourishing food" ended with famed Arctic explorer Vilhjalmur Stefansson. In an effort to prove the worth of the diet of the nomadic hunters and gatherers, Stefansson lived for over a year on nothing but meat and pemmican. Doctors who examined him after that period declared him to be in perfect health.[14]

If Stefansson's experience doesn't convince you of the benefit of pemmican, three Canadian adventurers provided more proof in early 2009 when they broke the world record for the fastest unassisted journey to the South Pole in Antarctica. Ray Zahab, Richard Weber and Kevin Vallely skied and snowshoed the more than 1130 kilometres from Hercules Inlet on the Ronne Ice Shelf to the South Pole in 33 days. They survived altitude sickness, enormous blisters, frozen snowdrifts and blinding whiteouts. According to the news reports that chronicled their journey, "They were powered by a 7000-calorie-per-day diet that included pemmican, butter and energy drinks."[15]

Modern technology may have contributed "energy drinks," but pemmican has stood the test of time. Victoria's "best and most nourishing food" won again!

How To Make Pemmican

Naomi McIlwraith is a writer employed as an Instructor/Researcher at the Faculty of Native Studies, University of Alberta. As a Historical Interpreter at Fort Edmonton Park for several seasons, Naomi learned to make pemmican and agreed to share her "pemmican experience" here. This piece is excerpted from a longer narrative that will be included in her Master's thesis, a creative study of the Plains Cree language and the reasons for its preservation.[16]

> You will need one really sharp and longish knife, a lot of practice, strong hands, a good sense of using a knife without slicing yourself. And it would help to have experienced tutelage from an old Cree lady, or a Dene lady, or an Ojibwa lady, or a Blackfoot lady, or an Apache lady…. I owe all my knowledge to three individuals, two whom I've met and one I have not. Olive Modersohn and Alice Harkness have worked at the Fort Edmonton Park Native Encampment for many years, and they taught me how to do this. I also credit Dr. Anne Anderson for the description in her book.
>
> You will also need a very large cutting board or a very large, flat cutting surface. The knife needs to be more than very sharp to make it easier for you to slice the buffalo meat into thin slices. Now, it doesn't have to be buffalo meat; it could be deer or moose or muskox or elk too, but I've made it with buffalo meat. Alice and her other sister, Mariah, are very good meat cutters, and they learned from their own mother and grandmother. I would say, based on my memory of doing this six or

seven years ago, to cut the meat about ☐ inch thick. I also remember that Mariah, who was especially good at cutting the meat, would study the meat very closely to determine the grain of it and then she would cut along that grain. Now, she would not cut right through the roast. She would stop cutting the meat maybe ☐ of an inch before cutting that slice right off, then she would turn the roast over and slice it through from that side. This way, the slices of meat would come off shaped almost like the two wings of a butterfly, each wing being about the size of one of my hands—palm and fingers included.

Okay, so now at this point the meat cutter must muster up as much patience as humanly possible in not getting too frustrated for the chunky, choppy results she or he might be getting. Slicing the meat as expertly as Mariah, Alice and Olive does take decades of experience. Keep slicing the meat as well as you can until you have it all sliced up. You should also have a large stainless steel bowl to place the meat slices in.

Once all the meat is sliced, you are ready for smoking and drying. Except, you will have prepared your tripod or meat-drying rack well in advance even of slicing the meat. For this very important phase in making "pimîhkân" (correct Cree spelling) you will need a large fire pit over which you will set your drying rack. Now before you bring the meat to the rack, it is very crucial that you build a large fire and let it burn into hot, hot coals. You will also need to have done considerable work gathering wood and chopping it into small firewood. You will need A LOT of small firewood, and it needs to be small because when you actually dry your meat, YOU DO NOT WANT A FIRE; YOU WANT A SMUDGE. I apologize for yelling in the printed word, but it is really important that the meat is SMOKED AND NOT COOKED. This is also why you need to burn a fire for a long time before actually smoking the meat, so that you can build up a very hot bed of coals on which to put the small firewood. When you smoke the meat, several conditions must exist. First, the fire cannot be a fire but a smudge. To make a smudge on your hot coals, you need to have gathered moss or punky wood from a decaying tree. *Birch is best, as the bark will hold together beautifully while the interior decays to punk.* You must smoke your meat only on a hot, sunny day. If it starts to rain, quickly gather up the meat, place a cloth over it, and run for cover. Two things will hasten the process of the dried meat going bad: heat and moisture.

Once you have a good smudge happening, place your meat slices carefully on your drying rack.

How long do you smoke the meat? For several days, as long as those days are hot and sunny and for as long as the day is long. I would say it takes about four or five days of smoking and drying until the meat is dried and brittle enough for pounding. As the meat smokes and dries, it will curl up and change from a bright red colour to a darker brownish colour. Keep drying and smoking until it is brittle enough to tear and break off into pieces.

Once all the meat is really dried and smoked, break it into quite small pieces, as small as a toonie or a loonie if you can manage it. You want to do this because it will facilitate pounding the meat into as fine a powder as you can. It's best to have a leather bag in which you put the meat, because all that pounding with a rock really takes a toll on the bag. For all our efforts at Fort Edmonton Park, we didn't have a leather bag so Alice made us two, thick canvas bags with special stitching so they wouldn't blow apart with the first blow. We had lots of help with the pounding, and we had little kids and big dads and strong moms pounding the meat with us. It really needs to be pounded an awful lot, about 10 times more than you will think it needs and about 20 times more than you will want to pound, because the finer the powder and the fewer the chunks the better the pimîhkân.

With your bowl of pounded meat—you will notice the quantity seems a whole lot less than the big roast you started with because the drying and smoking has evaporated all the moisture and reduced the size—prepare for the final stages of the making pimîhkân.

Try to do this in mid to late July when either the Saskatoons, or a little later, the choke-cherries, are ripe. Pick a bunch of berries and try not to eat too many. Dry them for a couple of days with your meat. Cheesecloth works good at the top of your drying rack. We constructed a little shelf up there with smaller sticks fastened onto the main branches of the tripod. Once your berries are dried, really dried, you can crush and grind them and pound them similarly to the way you make minced meat. If you use choke-cherries, it is okay to crush and grind the pits of the chokecherries, too.

Okay, so now you have dried and pounded meat and berries. You need one more ingredient: rendered buffalo fat or the fat of whatever kind of meat you've dried. That is one smelly job that stirs up quite a stink. Build another fire and get a big, cast iron pot that won't mind being used for rendering fat. Throw the fat into the pot and place the pot over the fire. This takes some time, too, as the fat needs to boil for awhile until the solid chunks separate. These solid chunks, by the way, will look and smell suspiciously like Kentucky Fried Chicken. As the fat cooks, remove the chunks. When the fat has cooked for quite some time and you're quite certain all the chunks have emerged that are supposed to, you have finished rendering the fat.

This is one job you will definitely want to do in clothes that you don't much care about.

Remember a ways back when I said there are two things you need to avoid in preparing pimîhkân? Heat and moisture. This means that when you add the fat to the meat and berries, you must LET IT COOL. Don't cool it so much that it starts to solidify again; just cool it so that it's tepid and you can touch it with your fingers. THE FAT

CANNOT BE HOT. Mix the crushed berries with the pounded meat first, and thoroughly. Now pour some cooled liquid fat onto this mixture. For the life of me, I can't say with any exactness what the quantities are. I will stress, however, that you don't want to overdo it with the fat because it will be too greasy. Basically put only enough cooled, liquid grease in until the meat and berry mixture starts to bind or stick together.

We had two responses to our pimîhkân, and I think I have made it three times: great interest or great distaste. You will either like it or not like it, and out of necessity, if you have to eat it for survival, you will grow to like it. I went to a real Ghost Dance at Kehewin First Nation about four years ago and I tasted their pimîhkân. I would say that my third effort at Fort Edmonton was very close to the pimîhkân I tasted at Kehewin.

Author's Note: An additional recipe for pemmican was included in a 1967 *Northern Cookbook* by Eleanor Ellis that simply stated, "Pound dried moose or deer meat on a piece of clean canvas or stone to fine crumbs. Pour hot melted moose fat over in pan. Let freeze. Serve cold. Very rich."[17] The instructions given by Naomi McIlwraith are much more authentic. And, of course, the Plains Cree or

Métis of Victoria's day would not have been able to freeze their pemmican.

References

1. MacEwan, Grant. "Victoria Callihoo: Granny." *And Mighty Women Too: Stories of Western Canadian Pioneers*. Prairie Books, 1975, 194.

2. Newman, Peter. C. *Caesars of the Wilderness*. Canada: Viking/Penguin Books, 1987, 43.

3. Ibid., 44.

4. Cruise, David, and Allison Griffiths. *The Great Adventure*. Penguin Canada, 1998, 235.

5. Ibid., 272.

6. Callihoo, Victoria. "Our Buffalo Hunts." *Alberta Historical Review*. Vol. 8, No. 1, 1960, 24–25.

7. Newman, *Caesars of the Wilderness*, 43.

8. Brink, Jack W. *Imagining Head-Smashed-In: Aboriginal Buffalo Hunting on the Northern Plains*. Edmonton: Athabasca University Press, 2008, 232.

9. Chodin, Tim, and Dan Asfar. *Gabriel Dumont: War Leader of the Métis*. Edmonton: Folklore Publishing, 2003, 17.

10. Brink, *Imagining Head-Smashed-In*, 234.

11. Ibid., 230.

12. Callihoo, "Our Buffalo Hunts," 25.

13. Brink, *Imagining Head-Smashed-In*, 232.

14. Ibid., 233.

15. "Canadians fastest to cross Antarctica." *Edmonton Journal*, January 8, 2009. http://www.edmontonjournalcom/Canadians+fastest+cross+Antarctica/1154271/story.html

16. McIlwraith, Naomi. Communication with the author February 2, 2009.

17. Ellis, Eleanor. *Northern Cookbook*. Ottawa: Indian Affairs and Northern Development, 1967.

Appendix 2—Red River Cart

WHEN I WAS A CHILD, my grandmother told me about the Red River cart she remembered from her childhood. The main description as far as she was concerned was the sound. "Screeching," she said, "like chalk on the blackboard. But so loud that you could hear it for miles."

The description stayed with me, and it wasn't until I was researching this article that I realized that Granny wasn't alone in that comparison. In Peter C. Newman's book on the fur trade, he notes, "the single axle was never greased because that would have attracted dust and grit, and the resultant noise was comparable to that of five thousand fingernails being drawn across a thousand blackboards."[1]

The Clay County Historical Society in Minnesota built their own Red River cart in 2000 and thoughtfully recorded the sound it made (see their website, for those of you who don't want to use fingernails or chalk on blackboards).[2]

Remember, when Victoria and her family travelled on those buffalo hunts, there were several hundred carts moving along together, not just one cart. It isn't likely that those who heard the sound all the time could ever ignore it, and for those who had never heard it before, it could be painful. One officer of the early North West Mounted Police described the "ox-cart concert" in his diary:

I would here like to describe the noise by the carts, but words fail me. It must be heard to be understood. A den of wild beasts cannot be compared with it in hideousness. Combine all the discordant sounds ever heard in Ontario and they cannot produce anything so horrid as a train of Red River carts. At each turn of the wheel, they run up and down all the notes of the scale in one continuous screech, without sounding distinctly any note or giving one harmonious sound.[3]

In their article "Traditional Métis Transportation," Prefontaine, Paquin and Young mention that there was even a belief among certain First Nations people that it was the sound of the Red River cart that drove the bison from the Canadian prairies![4]

Victoria mentions that they attempted to silence the squealing, shrieking sound of the cart by using tallow or grease. Unfortunately, although that might help, the sand and grit from the trail had a kind of sandpaper effect on the wheels and axles that caused them to wear out sooner.[5]

But despite the horrendous noise, the carts were an important factor in the settlement of the West. Unlike pemmican, which the Métis adapted from the local tribes, the Red River cart was a Métis invention. Like the birchbark canoe, the Red River

Red River cart and Métis driver (1874), artist Henri Julien

cart was a brilliantly practical means of transportation that could be built and maintained using the material at hand.

The first written reference of the Red River cart is found in the journals of fur trader Alexander Henry the younger in 1801,[6] and the earliest carts were small with solid wheels, three feet in circumference, made by slicing a large tree trunk. These early carts could carry up to 450 pounds. Unfortunately, they could easily be bogged down by mud on the trail, so larger, spoked wheels were developed.[7]

The standard Red River cart had a wooden box measuring two metres long, a metre high and half a metre wide, with axles two metres long. The two shafts, each measuring four metres long, ran from the box to the horse or oxen that would pull it.[8] Wooden pegs instead of nails were used so that any part of the cart that broke on the trail could easily be replaced at the nearest stand of trees.

Because the cart was completely constructed out of wood, it was also easy to remove the wheels and place them on top of the box of the cart in order to float the entire vehicle across streams or rivers that might be too deep to ford.[9]

One big advantage of the Red River cart was that it could carry the same weight of supplies as four packhorses. A cart pulled by a horse could manage 200 kilograms and travel nearly 80 kilometres in one day, whereas when pulled by oxen, the load could be up to 500 kilograms, but the oxen were only able to travel 30 kilometres per day. Often several teams were tied together so that one person could manage many loads. These "trains" of Red River carts were also less likely to get stuck in the mud than a single cart.[10]

One of the major routes for these "cart trains" was known as the Carlton Trail, which went from St. Boniface, Manitoba, via Fort Carlton on the North Saskatchewan River, eventually arriving at Fort Edmonton. According to Hudson's Bay Company records, an average of 300 carts per year made the trip carrying provisions and furs.[11]

And in spite of its commercial use, the Red River cart of Victoria's childhood might be called the equivalent of today's family car!

References

1. Newman, Peter. C. *Caesars of the Wilderness.* Canada: Viking/Penguin Books, 1987, 164.

2. "A Few Thoughts About Red River Carts." Clay County Historical Society Newsletter, March/April 2000. http://www.info.co.clay.mn.us/history/red_river_carts.htm

3. Cruise, David, and Allison Griffiths. *The Great Adventure.* Penguin Canada, 1998, 182.

4. Prefontaine, Darren R., Todd Paquin, and Patrick Young. "Traditional Métis Transportation." http://www.metismuseum.ca/media/document.php/00728.pdf

5. Hollihan, Tony. *Kootenai Brown*. Edmonton: Folklore Publishing, 2001, 122.

6. Métis Culture and Heritage Resource Centre— Red River Cart Building: http://www.metisresourcecentre.mb.ca/history/rrcartb.htm

7. Hollihan, *Kootenai Brown*, 122.

8. Prefontaine, Paquin, and Young, "Traditional Métis Transportation."

9. Newman, *Caesars of the Wilderness*, 164.

10. Prefontaine, Paquin, and Young, "Traditional Métis Transportation."

11. "Red River Cart" entry, The Encyclopedia of Saskatchewan http://esask.uregina.ca/entry/red_river_cart.html

Appendix 3—Tail Creek and Buffalo Lake

VICTORIA CALLIHOO REMEMBERED THAT some of the buffalo hunts she went on took them as far south as

Tail Creek.[1] Although today all that remains of the settlement is a marker near the coffee shop at Nevis by the bridge over the Red Deer River, in the mid 1800s, Tail Creek, or *Tail Creek des Métis*, was the largest town in western Canada.

At a time when Winnipeg and Vancouver were hardly considered towns, and St. Boniface was the largest centre in Manitoba with a population of 750, Tail Creek was a settlement with 2000 people.[2] It was the largest of the towns that were used as wintering places for the Métis buffalo hunters and their families. It covered an area on both sides of Buffalo Tail Creek and began as a place where buffalo hunters caught away from home by early winter storms made their temporary dwellings. Since some of these hunters came from as far away as the Red River area in Manitoba, it made sense for them to have homes nearer to their main source of food—the plains bison, or buffalo.

Unlike Victoria's home settlement at Lac Ste. Anne, Tail Creek and Buffalo Lake and the other smaller wintering towns were never considered permanent homes, despite the wishes of the Oblate priests who ministered to their religious beliefs. Each winter after the fall hunts, the hunters returned to the settlement, repaired their old cabin or built a new one. These were well-built, one-room log buildings, with dove-tailed corners, plastered and whitewashed inside.[3] They were similar to the cabin that was Victoria's home as a child.

Buffalo Lake was another settlement, and although not as large as Tail Creek, it was a winter home for many of the Métis who still pursued a nomadic life, following the buffalo and other game that was their source of food.

During the winter, the Métis people spent their time processing the hides they had harvested. They made harnesses for the Red River carts, saddles for their ponies, tipis and clothing for themselves. As well, the hides and pemmican were traded at the Hudson's Bay Company post at Edmonton.

Although there was plenty of hard work, the Métis hunters and their families knew how to celebrate. There was always a fiddler and dancers competing to see who could dance the Red River jig the fastest and the longest. Father Lacombe called the Métis "merry-making people,"[4] and he was right.

Come spring, the Métis men and their families abandoned the little cabins as they pursued the herds of buffalo that moved north for the lush spring grasses. They spent the summer pitching their tipis wherever game led them, just as their Native ancestors had done before them.

Like any town or city that gets its livelihood from one particular "industry," Tail Creek and the other winter settlements died when the great buffalo herds disappeared from the Prairies. By 1898, prairie fires had all but destroyed the town of Tail Creek. One cabin was taken to Stettler to be preserved as a memorial.[5]

According to the federal census in 1901, only 91 descendants of the original buffalo hunters remained living in Tail Creek.[6] Soon all that was left of the bustling town was the cemetery and perhaps the echo of fiddle music haunting the night winds along the banks of Buffalo Tail Creek.

Tail Creek Cemetery

References

1. Callihoo, Victoria. "Our Buffalo Hunts." *Alberta Historical Review.* Vol. 8, No. 1, 1960, 24.

2. The Métis in Alberta, "The People of Tail Creek":
   http://www.albertasource.ca/METIS/eng/peo-
   ple_and_communities/tail_creek-people.htm

3. The Métis in Alberta, "Buffalo Lake and Tail
   Creek":
   http://www.albertasource.ca/METIS/eng/peo-
   ple_and_communities/historic_ buffalo_lake.
   htm

4. Macpherson, Elizabeth. *The Sun Traveller: The
   Story of the Callihoos in Alberta*. Edmonton. Musée
   Héritage Museum St. Albert, 42.

5. Taylor, Cora. "Buffalo Hunters of Tail Creek."
   Celebrating Alberta: Many Places. Don Mills, ON:
   Pearson Education Canada, 2007, 13.

6. The Métis in Alberta, "The People of Tail
   Creek."

Appendix 4—Whiskey Trade

ONE OF THE MOST TRAGIC RESULTS of the arrival of the
white man on the North American plains was that
the whiskey traders arrived before the missionaries
or settlers. By the 1870s they were consistently
crossing the "Medicine Line," as the border between
Canada and the United States was called, bartering

their poisonous brew with tribes in Alberta. The liquor the whiskey traders traded caused great hardship for the Native people, particularly the Peigan, Blood and Blackfoot who lived in southern Alberta.[1]

The alcohol that caused so many problems for the Blackfoot Confederacy became known as "firewater" because it flared up when the whiskey traders poured it into the campfire. The Native customers believed that they were getting the real thing, whiskey.

Although they were known as "whiskey traders," very little actual whiskey was dispersed. It's hard to believe that anyone could drink the concoction that was traded at that time. Some of the recipes for this firewater have been recorded. In 1872 the brother of the lieutenant-governor of Manitoba visited some traders on the Montana border of Alberta. Curious as to what was causing the tribes he had visited to behave so violently after they had been drinking the trade whiskey, he tasted some. It was so awful that after one sip his lips burned and tears rolled down his cheeks. "What's in it?" he gasped.

The traders roared with laughter and explained how they had made it. First they boiled tobacco and lake water into a foul-smelling dark brown soup then they added high-proof alcohol and several pounds of blue vitriol or sulphuric salts. Blue vit, they explained, was the secret ingredient that gave the "whiskey" a powerful afterburn—few white men could get it past their lips.[2]

Recipes for the whiskey varied from place to place, and the traders could be very creative when the need arose. Usually the brew contained a combination of four parts water to one part whiskey, but it was the additives that probably caused most of the trouble. The mixture had to flame up to be proper "firewater." Burnt sugar and oil was added to give it colour and flammability. Bourbon, which was cheaper, was often substituted for whiskey. Other ingredients that might be added were paint (obviously not for flavour but to add colour and to make it flammable), ginger (to add flavour and kick), molasses (the dark colour counteracted all the water that was added, so it looked like whiskey as well as provided some sweetness), red pepper (again, for kick) and patent medicines. Patent medicine at that time often contained alcohol as well as having a very strong flavour.[3]

On one occasion recorded at Fort Peigan in 1831, after trading all but one 35-gallon keg of whiskey, 1000 Blackfoot warriors arrived at the fort demanding trade in firewater. To appease the warriors, the whiskey trader added all the patent medicine he had on hand (usually foul-tasting remedies for stomach upset). He then put in red peppers, black-strap molasses, tobacco and all the red ink he could find. By adding a lot of water, he ended up with 350 gallons of whiskey.[4]

It is no wonder that those who drank the fire-water became violently inebriated and were often very sick afterwards. A firewater hangover was a dreadful thing.

The whiskey trade was destructive to the local tribes but very lucrative to the traders, who often made over $50,000 in furs in a single trip north.[5]

References

1. Cruise, David, and Allison Griffiths. *The Great Adventure. Penguin* Canada, 1998, 28.

2. Ibid., 109.

3. Ibid., 105.

4. Ibid., 106.

5. Ibid.

Appendix 5—Michif Language

THE STORY GOES THAT THE FIRST time Victoria Callihoo used a telephone to call her daughter, she worried that she would have to speak English. She was delighted to find the machine would work when she used her "own language."

Although Victoria might not have known it, the language she spoke ("her own language") was probably what is now known as Michif. She would have thought she was speaking Cree or a mixture of French and Cree. Métis people of her time were not aware that they were creating and speaking a new language—one that those who study linguistics today consider unique in its construction and usage.

One of Canada's foremost experts on the Michif language, Professor Robert A. Papen of the Departement de linguistique et didactique des langues, Université du Québec à Montréal, told me that it is not actually known when the Métis started calling their language "Michif." Evidently in St. Laurent, Manitoba, the older people still refer to their language as "French," but it is referred to as "Michif" by the younger folks—people in their 60s! However, Professor Papen explained that the term "Michif" simply means "Métis," and is in fact the local pronunciation of the word *metif* or *mitif*, which was the term originally used in New France instead of the word "métis" that is used today.[1] Just as Cree people would say they spoke Cree, the Métis are in fact saying they speak Métis.

The earliest Métis probably spoke a mixture of French and Ojibwe/Salteaux. Later as the fur traders moved farther west, the descendants of the voyageurs who came to western Canada with the fur trade and married Cree women created the mixture of French and Cree that became the Michif language. Today, probably only a thousand or more people speak Michif, and they are scattered throughout Saskatchewan, Manitoba and northern Alberta as well as some in North Dakota and Montana.

Although it uses a mixture of Cree verbs and French nouns, the language developed independently. And although the language may have been originally created by people who were bilingual in French and Cree, many Michif speakers today are unable to speak Cree and only a few speak French.[2]

On my visit to the Batoche Historic Site in Saskatchewan, Mark Calette, the director, mentioned that his grandmother referred to the language as "our talk."

In his book *A Language of Our Own*, Peter Bakker discusses the "problem of Michif" and how this original North American language does not fit into any of the categories linguists use to arrange languages into a language family.[3] To begin with, Michif is a half Cree (an Amer-Indian) and half

French (a European, Romance) language. As well, it is not a case of it being a pidgin type of language where people who speak two different languages invent a simplified language using words from both in order to communicate. Nor is it a Creole type of language where one language is dominant. And unlike trade languages, used when people have to communicate with those of other languages, Michif is not spoken to those who do not understand it.

In Michif, Cree verbs, personal pronouns and demonstratives are used, whereas nouns, articles and numerals are always French. To further complicate matters, Michif verbs have the same complexity as Cree verbs, but Michif nouns are used and categorized in the French way. In addition, the order in which the words are used follows the structure of the Cree language, but noun phrases follow that of the French language.

Adjectives come only from French since Cree does not have adjectives. Interestingly, adjectives that come before the noun (*une belle fille, une beau garçon*) agree in gender (either masculine or feminine), but those that come after the noun (*une maison vert, un char vert*) do not.[4]

When Cree words are used, they are structured as they would be in Cree, and French words are structured in the French way.

In most cases, where there is a mixture of two languages, one will be dominant. Not so with the Michif language; it is not a case of French borrowing from Cree, or Cree borrowing from French. Usually with language mixtures there will be a combined vocabulary, and the pronunciation of the dominant language is adapted but in Michif, both of the root languages (Cree and French) follow their own sound system. In that matter, too, it is unique in the world of linguistics.

Attempts have been made to explain the origins of the Michif language by suggesting that Cree verbs and French nouns developed because Cree (the language of the women who married the French-speaking voyageurs) contains words that had to do with the work the women usually did (thus verbs or "action" words were Cree), and the men (the French speakers) provided the nouns by pointing at objects and naming them. Although an amusing theory, it is immediately debunked by examining some of the words in the Michif language. For example, the word for "berry picking" (usually a woman's task) in Michif is Cree and the names for the various types of berries are French might reinforce the theory, though many other words do not. However, the word for "shooting" (verb) is Cree, and the word for "gun" (noun) is French. Obviously the verb "shooting" doesn't relate to "women's work" in that case. And words that relate to things that both men and women did, such as "eating" and "sleeping," or words that describe objects in the home that both might use, adhere to the general rule of verbs being Cree while nouns were French regardless of who was "eating the food."[5]

Exceptions to this might be words such as "pemmican" or "muskeg"—nouns for which there was no French word and so the Cree word was adopted.

Bakker states that Michif seems to be "an impossible language," one that many "professional linguists claim cannot exist." No wonder Michif is found to be unique in the world of linguistics![6]

The Métis of western Canada created a complex, completely unusual language. The Michif language developed in a unique time and place, part of the growth of the identity of the Métis people of Canada, and Victoria's amazing life, from her birth in 1861 to her death in 1966, spanned that remarkable development.

References

1. Papen, Robert A. Communication with the author February 11, 2009.

2. Bakker, Peter. *A Language of Our Own: The Genesis of Michif, the Mixed Cree-French Language of the Canadian Métis.* Oxford University Press, 1997, 1.

3. Ibid., 3.

4. Papen, Robert A.

5. Bakker, *A Language of Our Own*, 16.

6. Ibid., 3.

Appendix 6—Family Tree (Belcourts and Callihoos)

THE FOLLOWING PAGES LIST THE family tree of the Belcourt and Callihoo families as well as a list of Victoria's descendants. In some cases the full information (e.g., date of death, full names and so on) is not known.

Children of Nancy and Alexis Belcourt (Victoria's parents)

Sophie (1849–1934)

Alexander (1852–1915)

Christianne (1855–1953)

Louisa (1858–?) married John Horatio Nelson Brazeau

Victoria Anne (1861–1966)

Athanese (1865–70)

Virginie (1867–?) obviously grew up as she married twice

Joseph (1871–88)

John (1875–?) obviously grew up as he married

Mary Jane Euphasine (1882–?)

Elizabeth Finlay (adopted) (1877–?); obviously grew up as she married twice

The Children and Grandchildren of Louis Jerome Callihoo and Victoria Belcourt Callihoo

Anne (1879–1969) married Stoney Boris

Philomene Marie Anne (1904–83) m. Wilfred Letendre (1896–1971)

Ida Boris (b. 1913–?)

Nora May Boris (b. 1915–?) m. Edward "Buck" Callihoo (1908–78)

Albert Daniel Boris (1919–64) m. Ellen Arnold

John Henry Boris (1921–?)

Anne then married Jean Baptiste Loyer (1883–?) with whom she had one child, Louis Daniel Loyer (1908–?). (It's unclear what happened to Stoney Boris. There's no date of death for him, but when I was at the Alberta Beach Museum I found a mention of the Boris family in the local history book,

Spirit Trails of Lac Ste. Anne. Evidently, according to the write-up, Stoney Boris had disappeared "...after having an auction sale he took off to Washington for a job and was never heard from.")

Dio Leon (1880–1944?)

Hermine "Lizzie" (1881–1976) married Benjamin Vandelle/Vandal (1893–1976)

Ernest Clarence (b. 1914)

Louise Vandelle m. Robert Hope

Marie Vandelle (b. 1917) m. Meili

Alice Vandelle (b. 1918) m. Lou McClure

Phillip Vandelle (b. 1920)

Buster Vandelle

Louisianna Vandelle m. Andrew McLure

Rose Vandelle m. Wood (no first name given)

Bill Vandelle

Delia Vandelle m. Dan Pitner

Raymond Vandelle m. Nancy Nibbs

Norman Vandelle m. Edith/Ida Dion

William J. (1881–1954) married Anne English (1883–1910) and had one child, Patrice Callihoo.

m. Anne Gairdner (1906–97)

Herbert Allen m. Joan Ford

Patricia (1926–?) m. Ron Robinson

Adolphus (1885–1967) married Christine Breland (1890–1973) div.

Modeste "Matt" (1911–93) m. Nora Letendre

Clara (Mable) (1913–96) first husband Francis Labonte; second husband Stan Havig

Napoleon (1916–?) first wife Violet Parris; second wife Shelley

Therese Irene (1919–?) m. Matt Shaefer

Alex Montrose (1925–87) m. Beatrice Gladys Callihoo (1922–?)

Florence Elizabeth

Elsie

Jerome

m. Louise Bellerose

Billy Dolphus (1911–?)

David (1915–?)

Doris

Edith

Kenneth

m. Eliza (no record of last name)

Gloria Margaret Rose (1939–?)

Mildred

Vital Victor (1888–1972) married Clothilde Maria Hodgson (1897–1983)

George (1918–98) m. Irene Bell and Francis

Lucy (1919–?) m. Norman Cooper

Julie (1921–?) m. Al Hagget

Anne (1922–?) m. George Goerz

Pierre Paul (1925–?) m. Octavie L'Hirondelle (1928–?)

Dio Daniel (b.? –1966) m. Bernice Cormier

Therese m. Derek Vanoss and Jack ?

Olive m. Walter Matthews

Jane m. Ron Ferguson and ? Emslie

Louis Gilbert (1934–1934)

David (1939–?) m. Hillary

Walter m. Shirley Rolls

Winnifred

Henry (1889–1939) married Clara Hazel Loyer (b.?–1974)

Alma m. Alex Shennan

Ella m. Armond Guenette

Wilfred (1938–?) m. Gladys L'Hirondelle (1939–?)

Wilbert/Wilbur m. Marion Webber (b.?–1983)

Gordon (1939– ?) m. Muriel Sieb (1942–?)

Gilbert m. Barbara Whitwick

Alvina ("Alice") (1895–1975) married Charles Baird

Lillian ("Lily") May (1912–2001) m. Bert Ogden

Ben (1915–?)

George (1916–?)

Rose (1918–?) m. Ivor Swanson

Julie Mary (1920–?)

Victorine Laura (1921–?)

Joseph (1923–1923)

Joan (1936–?) m. Albert Leonard Abbot (1933–?)

James

Grace m. S. Doodar

Alvin

Judy m. Bill Phillips

Violet m. Francis Berube

Ivy m. Leonard Forcade

Jean m. Don Kilpatrick

Caroline (1897–1897)

Melvina (1897–1898)

John (1898–1915)

Julia Mary ("May") (1901–?) married Wilfred John Laderoute/Seguin (1897–1989)

Edna m. Bill Wahlen

Aileen m. Dan Tate

Clifford

Evelyn m. George Livingstone

Teresa m. Rollie Moen

Verna m. Warren Watson

Elinor m. Wayne McCullough

Shirley m. George Greyschuk

Dorothy m. Art Perkins

John Wilfred

Bertha Victoire ("Vickie") (1903–?) married Roderick Letendre (1900–?) in 1922.

m. Larry Dennis

Stanley James Dennis (1934–?)

m. F. Kildaw

References

Macpherson, Elizabeth. *The Sun Traveller: The Story of the Callihoos in Alberta*. St. Albert, AB: Musée Héritage Museum, 2003.

Métis Genealogical Records, Musée Héritage Museum, St. Albert, Alberta.

Appendix 7—Victoria's Memories

WHEN VICTORIA WAS 91, the following stories were dictated and translated into English. They were published in the *Alberta Historical Review* and the *St. Albert Gazette,* and some of them were reprinted in the Lac Ste. Anne Historical Society's local history book *West of the Fifth* as well as in Herb Belcourt's *Walking in the Woods* and Emeric Drouin's *Lac Ste. Anne Sakahigan.*

The stories are reprinted here with the permission of the *Alberta Historical Review*.

~~~~~~~~~

Callihoo, Victoria. "Early Life in Lac Ste. Anne and St. Albert in the 1870s." *Alberta Historical Review*. Vol. 1, No. 3, 1953, 21–26.

Our houses were made of hewn spruce logs mostly. We had only two windows in them, no upper floors, no glass, but a rawhide skin of a calf, deer or moose calf was used. Only the hair would be taken off. It was put on the window while wet, and nailed on with wooden pegs on slats around the window. When dry it would be taut and might be used as a drum. It was not transparent, but gave light. Though not as good as glass, it had one advantage, no Peeping Tom was going to peep through your window. Therefore, window blinds were unnecessary.

We had saws about eight feet long—they looked like ice saws—with handles at each end. A platform was built about ten feet above the ground. A log would be hoisted up and a man on top would pull the saw up, the man below would pull down, sawing the log on the downward stroke. Lots of floors were made of hewn logs. All the tools were supplied by the Hudson's Bay Company store. Rafters were made of poles about three feet apart. Most of the roofs were one-quarter pitch. Then the builder would go into the forest to get bark from the spruce trees, the bark being taken off the trees during sapping time. The length of the bark would be six feet or so and the width vary according to the size of the tree. This bark, after it was taken off the tree, would be set flat on rails above the ground to dry. I may say now that the very best of timber was within a mile from the settlements for there were no loose fires in those days to destroy and mar nature's picture. When the bark was dry in the fall, it was then laid on the rafters, lapping on top like shingles. The bark was then pinned down with long poles crosswise from the roof. Holes were bored in pole and pins made of wood were driven tight, thus making a leakproof roof. The outer bark was laid outside. The inside roof was therefore smooth and glossy.

As there were no stoves, open fireplaces were built in either corner from the door. We called these mud stoves. They were made of poles, mud and hay mixed, and more mud and water making a smooth finish. White clay was then mixed with water and rubbed all over with a cloth. When dry this was white. Usually two iron bars were hung about four feet from the floor. These bars were used to hang kettles on. We got these bars from the Hudson's Bay Company and also from old, discarded guns. About a foot away from the mud stove the floor was plastered down solid, a precaution taken so sparks would not ignite and burn the house. The open chimney was built about two feet above the roof, so the sparks would not drop on the roof. On a windy night, sparks could be seen coming out thick, but the chimney being high they would drop on the ground harmlessly. The house was then chinked, plastered with clay, white-mud washed, a cellar door was made in the floor and the house was ready to move into.

But before the house had been occupied two days, the owner had to invite the neighbours to a big dance. We danced reels, jigs and other dances. We had no tables; because we didn't have them we didn't miss them; no chairs or benches. We ate on the floor. A canvas was spread with a white cloth on top; then set ready for the meal. We had a three-cornered cupboard in a corner for our dishes. A cloth was hung over, for lumber was scarce and hard to make. We got strap-hinges and latches from the Posts. Others had wooden latches and wooden hinges. A hole was bored in a slab or board and another slab with a tongue in the end, would serve as a hinge. They were very squeaky. Our pots and dishes were from the Hudson's Bay Company store. The pots were made of copper and seamless. We had eight-gallon to two-pint pots. They were very useful and stood rough usage.

When a pot was bumped it was easy to hammer back to its proper shape.

There were no beds; everyone slept on the floor. All bedding was gathered, folded and placed in one corner of the house in the day time. At night big pieces of slab wood would be placed, standing up (perpendicular), on the mud stove. Usually, coals of fire would still be burning in the morning. The fire from the mud stove would give a glow, providing both heat and light. We had no lamps nor candles, so after a few years we made our own candles. Our bedding consisted of duck and goose feathers for mattresses and pillows, and buffalo robes and Hudson's Bay Company four-point blankets.

We had no flour. We grew a little barley. We cut a block of black poplar about 30 inches high and 16 inches in diameter. We bored a hole about 8 inches deep and 7 inches across. We would soak the barley in lukewarm water for awhile, drain off the water, and pour the barley into this block. We had a hammer-like apparatus that just fitted this, with which we pounded the barley in the hole for about twenty minutes. In that time the hulls would be all off the grain. We separated the hulls from the grain and used the grain for soup which was wholesome and delicious. When the grain was very dry, we put it in a frying-pan adding a little grease, and when cooked brown it was a good substitute for bread. We had no coffee, but again barley came to the rescue. We put the barley in the frying pan, without hulling it, and when it was fried real black we used that for coffee. We had tea and block sugar like we had during the war in the cafes.

Though the buffalo had now gone, we raised cattle hogs and chickens. Food was still plentiful and moose, deer, and bear were plentiful. We then turned to these animals for food and clothing. Moose hide when tanned made nice moccasins and coats, pants, mitts, gloves and other articles, but it never made a robe—the hair came off too easily, and the same with deer. We began raising cattle and, in the fall we butchered one, or sometimes two, to carry us through the winter. Some of the Metis didn't care for beef at first, but they soon got over that.

We got thread from the Hudson's Bay Company store and we learned to make our nets. We had lots of fish—we were never short of food.

We milked cows. We made our own milk pans out of birchbark. We used tiny, long roots which we got in the muskegs to sew the pans and berry pots with. We used spruce gum heated to close the seams and leaks of the birch pans. Birch canoes were made the same way. They were very light.

We barbequed fish, fowl and large pieces of meat over the open fire. Or covered the bird, feathers and all under hot coals of wood, and this cooked beautifully, and you ate something that was never touched by anyone. Potatoes were cooked the same way and had good flavour.

Our clothing was from cloth brought by the Hudson's Bay Company. Our men never wore underwear, nor socks—there weren't any—but we had large overcoats from buffalo skins and outer leggings were worn, made from Hudson's Bay Company blankets. These leggings reached up to the waist. A buckskin string was tied to the legging and that tied to one's belt. Women also had no stockings. Like the men, they wrapped their feet with an oblong piece of flannel. Women wore leggings. They were worn below the knee. They were made of black velvet and were beaded on one side, the outside of the leg. When we women did outside work, or made trips in winter, we wrapped our knees with flannelette. Women had no coats, but wore shawls.

Our livestock consisted of horses, cattle, pigs and chickens, all scrubs.

During the buffalo hunts, some settler would go on through to Red River for supplies that weren't available here. They would bring back ploughs, garden tools and tubs. They would return in the fall and usually two families or more would come back with them to settle here. These families came in wagons. (Firewater) whiskey would be brought in from Winnipeg, and rum and brandy were sold or bartered by the Hudson's Bay Company.

We had no soap, but we made *la potash* from fats and grease with ashes and lye. We used it for our toilet and washing soap. Perhaps it was rather hard for the delicate skin, but it was as good as any soap I have used. Some of us still use *la potash* to this day.

No brooms were to be had at the store. We made them out of a certain kind of willow. We chose the long taper kind. These sticks were taken from the tops about two feet long. About one hundred of these would be tied together around a four-foot smooth stick—this was the broom handle. The stick was driven into the centre of the tied willows, and our broom was ready for use.

Moss was pulled up in the fall, after haying. Little spruce trees were cut half-way, about two feet from the ground, and the upper part pushed down, and we put our moss on top of this sort of rack, where it would dry before winter set in. It was hauled in as needed. Moss was a household necessity. We raised our babies with it. We stuffed it in moss bags in which our babies were laced up. We did not use any diapers. We used moss to wipe floors after scrubbing them.

We cultivated our land—an acre or two—with a ten-inch plough. An ox would be trained to pull it. The ox was used around the place and for hauling hay, but the ponies were used for fast travelling, such as going to weddings and dances, and in case of sickness, to get the priest. When ploughing was done a wooden harrow was then dragged on the ploughed land, usually a boy leading the horses. The seeds were sown broadcast. Fences were made of rails laid on blocks. The oxen and horses were driven singly. We had no double harness.

Our hogs were spotted, black and white. They were brought by boat up river by the Hudson's Bay Company. Our haying equipment was an Armstrong mower (scythe), wooden forks with wooden prongs, which were rather cumbersome. When the hay was dry, it was gathered with the forks and cocked. We had no hay rakes. When all the hay was cocked, it was left to settle for a few days, and it was brought in by two men with two poles. These poles were shoved under the cock about two feet apart, then the whole cock would be lifted clean and brought to the stack. Round hay stacks were put up. We had no hay racks. Small racks were built on long- runner sleighs, sort of a stone box. Oxen hauled the hay home in winter.

Of course, we had dog trains too, for faster trips. One didn't care when one left for a trip with a dog team, morning, noon or evening. My husband left Lac St. Anne in the evening and arrived at the "House," Edmonton, before sunrise the following morning.

After the hunts were over, some people went down to Morley or *Man-a-chap-pan-nihh* (meaning "where the bows are taken"). This is how Bow River got its name, which is wrong. Bow River in Indian is *Ask-ka-we-see*-pee, which means "Don't-freeze-over-river"; this river was never known to be frozen over all winter for ponies crossing it.

Better and cheaper horses were later brought up from the Blackfoot of the Old Man's River.

We bartered our furs at the Hudson's Bay Company. Usually the Company advanced a settler with credit after haying, and on through the year until the trapper brought in his catch. Often the fur would more than pay the debt the settler owed and the store would owe him. He would draw this off and on. As there was no money; this transaction was called "fur." So much fur for this, and so much fur for the other article. Later on, when the Indian Commissioners came to pay Treaty Money (late 1870s), money began to circulate. It seemed more confusing to deal with money when one was accustomed to barter. I have heard of some Indians trading a used five-dollar bill for a brand-new dollar bill.

Metis from Lac Ste. Anne and St. Albert often visited each other, that is, once or twice a year. These two settlements were of the same people, and they were related mostly. There would be a man or a family from Lac La Biche or Slave Lake who would come and live in the settlement. The two settlements were all Catholics: L'Hirondelle, Belcourt, Gladus, Plante, Laderoute and Gauthier, were of French descent. Letendres' ancestors came from the Beaver Indians in the Peace country; around forty years ago a lot of these people went up to Grande Prairie where trapping and hunting was good.

We went to see the Battle River people, off and on. Since they were Métis of French extraction like us, good fellowship prevailed, and some marriages took place. We did not come in contact with the Métis in Victoria; they being of Anglo-Saxon descent and a different denomination, no visits, to my knowledge, were ever made to them.

Definitions

Armstrong mower: a scythe (which is a long blade on the end of a handle). It is swung using the person's "strong arms."

Broadcast: a method of seeding where grain is thrown in a wide arc by hand.

Cocked: refers to the way that hay was built into a little stack or cock.

House (Edmonton): fur trading posts were often referred to as "houses"; for example, "Edmonton House" and "Rocky Mountain House."

Posts: Hudson's Bay Company trading post or store.

Scrubs: refers to livestock that is not purebred/pedigreed.

Stone box: a stone box or stone boat was a flat bed of logs or planks on runners that was used for loading stones when clearing land for cultivation.

Callihoo, Victoria. "The Iroquois in Alberta." *Alberta Historical Review.* Vol. 7, No. 2, 1959, 17–18.

I am telling this story as told to me by my late husband Louis Callihoo and also his father, Batiste, the latter being a son of Callihoo, one of the two first Iroquois to come out in this Western country. Bernard was the other man who also came out as voyageur for the Hudson's Bay Company. As near as I can reckon they came at least 125 years ago from Québec.

As voyageurs for the Hudson's Bay Company they sailed from Montréal down a river, perhaps Albany, to Moose Factory on James Bay. Then north westward on the Hudson's Bay to York Factory, on up the Nelson River into Lake Winnipeg, up the

North Saskatchewan to *Wask-ka-nee-win* (The House) Edmonton. This trip would start early in spring in Montréal and reach Edmonton in the fall. If the season was not late the men would go overland to (The Landing) Athabasca Landing where other boats were used, then up the Athabasca, Little Slave River and Lesser Slave Lake where these Iroquois worked and trapped for the Hudson's Bay Company and made their home.

In practically all the posts of the Hudson's Bay Company in the west, French was the language spoken. Perhaps this is accounted for by the fact that there were more Frenchmen among the voyageurs than other nationalities. I may say here that the Natives called the Frenchmen *mis-tick-oosee-wak* (wooden boats men) as they were the first people the Natives saw to use a boat other than a birch canoe, hence the name.

Bernard and Callihoo both were married. Who their wives were, or where they were from, is unfortunately unknown today. I am inclined to think these two men brought their wives with them.

I knew my husband's brothers and sisters. They were of larger stature and lighter skinned than the Cree. Bernard had a daughter only and she died in early womanhood. Callihoo had four sons, Michel, who lived to be 85 years and died in 1918, and Tama who died in middle life, and Batiste, who was the last one alive and was 78 when he died. The youngest boy, I now cannot recollect his name, was drowned at Fort Assiniboine on his way to Lesser Slave Lake. Callihoo, the original died in middle life and apparently Bernard took charge of his widow and children for they all came down to live at Lac Ste. Anne, at least the Callihoos did. Bernard, later in life was kept by the Sisters at St. Albert. He was a big powerfully built man, stood all of six feet at the time of his death. He, it is said, was 100 years old. I remember seeing him as does my son Bill, who was about thirteen years old then.

There were five girls in the first Callihoo family. The oldest girl married a Monsieur Belrose, a Frenchman who had charge of the Hudson's Bay post at Lac La Nonne. Later, he left the Company's employ and started a farm on the Sturgeon River a little ways east from St. Albert mission. Another girl married Pierre Delorme, also of St. Albert. The third girl married Batiste Belcourt of Lac St. Anne. The fourth girl married Joe Grey—this man was not a native here. He was a well-built man, fearless. He once met a grizzly face-to-face with a muzzle loader, stood his ground and killed the silver tip. He spoke with an accent like a Chippewa and died in Montana. The youngest girl married Laver Loyer of Lac St. Anne, who later farmed west of Big Lake west of St. Albert.

The sons, Michel and Batiste, both stood over six feet and were broad-shouldered and erect. Like the custom of the last era both wore their hair below the ears and above the neck. When Lord Aberdeen, who was Governor General of Canada toured the west accompanied by Lady Aberdeen, the Natives were called to meet them at Stony Plain Indian Agency (now Winterburn). As Michel and Batiste shook hands with His Excellency, he was struck with their stature and, turning to the Indian Agent, Count De Cauze, remarked, "these men are not of the Cree tribe." De Cauze replied, "No, they are not Cree they are Iroquois."

A few other Iroquois came west later and some of them went up the Athabasca River to Yellow Head Post where they worked for the Hudson's Bay Company. Wianda and Gauthier are the only names I can remember now. Quite a few of the descendants of these two live at Entrance. Among us people we know them as the Rocky Mountain people.

Perhaps it will not be amiss to add that the name Callihoo may live a long time. A little town west of Edmonton bears that name. A lake and a creek in the Grande Prairie country also bear that same name.

The following material also came from Victoria and is included in the local history book *West of the Fifth*.

There was a stockade at Lac Ste. Anne, but not so high was at Edmonton. There were lots and lots of dogs all over the settlement and the stockade was erected to bar them from the trading post and warehouse. The dog was used for transportation and hunting and easily raised; horses were very scarce and used mostly in summer when feed was abundant. The Hudson's Bay Company hired a woman to snare and deliver the rabbits for dog feed, a daily chore. She rode her pony out to her snare line, then packed the cayuse with the rabbits and led it home. The woman's husband wasn't very ambitious so she had to cut hay with the "arm strong" mower to feed the pony in winter. Willow wood crotches were used for hay forks until later when steel forks came, minus handles. The woman was Mrs Wiandi, an Iroquois.

Note: Mrs. Callihoo told her son William about the stockade, and he gave this information to the archivist of the Lac Ste. Anne Historical Society.

Callihoo, Victoria. "Our Buffalo Hunts." *Alberta Historical Review.* Vol. 8, No. 1, 1960, 24–25.

I was thirteen years old when I first joined in a buffalo hunt. We left Lac Ste. Anne after the leaves were out on the poplar trees and our small fields and gardens were seeded or planted. Before making the journey, there would be a meeting among the leading men as to the exact day of leaving. After this was decided on, all the families who wanted to join the hunt would prepare for the trip. Our main transportation, the Red River cart, would be overhauled. These vehicles at the time did not have any metal in their construction. Large wooden pegs were used where bolts would be used now, while small pegs answered for screws or nails. Cart harness was made of hides from buffalo.

I always used to accompany my mother on these trips. She was a medicine woman who set broken bones and knew how to use medicinal herbs. The riders who chased the buffalo were often thrown, sometimes by the bulls charging the riders' horses or by the horses getting their feet in badger holes.

We usually took three carts along. We had no axle grease, and tallow was used instead to lubricate the wooden axles. The carts were very squeaky and could be heard from a long way off.

We, from Lac Ste. Anne, would be the first to start as we were the furthest north. The Métis of

St. Albert settlement would join us on the way. Usually, there would be about one hundred families going on the hunt. All the streams were forded, as there were no bridges. The Saskatchewan River was the largest and most dangerous, and it was a relief after it was crossed. We used to cross at a good ford about where the High Level Bridge is now. About a day's travel south from Saskatchewan River, we usually found the herd. Riders, young men they were, would scout on ahead to see we did not run into any enemies. There were no police—no law. We always had a leader in our caravan, and his orders were respected. He always had a flag flying on top of his cart. He led his people ahead and we followed him.

When the herd was startled, it was just a dark solid moving mass. We, of those days, never could believe the buffalo would ever be killed off, for there were thousands and thousands. We took firewood and poles for tipis and for tripods, on which we hung our thin sliced slab meat to dry in the sun. We had no matches but got our fire from flint and birch punk. It seems no one was anxious to start their morning fire, as we would wait and see if any smoke would come out of the tipis, and when smoke was seen, then there was a rush to get a flame or coal to start one's own fire.

The riders of the chase all had guns, single barrel flint locks—some muzzle-loaders with caps. Bows and arrows were used before my time, but the Crees and Blackfoot still used them. Powder horns and ball rags were slung on each shoulder. At close range the guns would kill the animal. Some riders rode bareback, while others had homemade saddles. They were almost flat and were stuffed with the hair of the buffalo. They were beaded on the corners, and stirrups were of dry rawhide. When the kill was over, the women would go out to help bring the meat in, and then the slicing of the meat began. We girls would then keep a little smoke going all day to keep the flies away from the meat. The meat would be on rails that rested on two tripods on each end.

Often we would run short of wood. Then a pony would be hitched to a cart and we would go out on the plain and pick chips (buffalo dung). On a warm day, this was very dry and burned readily. Only the old ones were used for fuel. The buffalo was a very useful animal, for we ate the meat, we used its hide for robes, shelter for our lodges, footwear, clothes, and bags. The meat was cooked and sun-dried and also made into pemmican. We always camped close to water. We set our tipis in a large circle outside the cart circle. A few of the fastest horses were kept in this enclosure, and the others were herded all night by a night herder, for horse thieving was a very common occurrence. A fast horse was the best possession. A hunter on a fast horse would kill more buffalo than others with less speedy ponies. There was no money; no one knew what it was.

We made pemmican out on the plains, as the dried meat was too bulky to take home. A large green hide would be hung on six posts, three on each side, so the hide would form a U-shape. When it was dry, the slabs of meat would be dumped in the U-shaped hide and two men on each end would then pound the dry meat into a pulp. Then sun-dried saskatoons would be mixed and grease would be poured on and stirred to make an even mixture. When this was done, it would be packed in robes, sewn with sinew all around, the hair part outside to keep the pemmican in good condition regardless of the weather. These bags were heavy, and it usually took two men to load one on a cart. Hides would be put on top of the loads. Nothing was wasted from the buffalo but the bones, hoofs and horns. The fall hunt, the last before winter, which would start after haying, was the most important one, for we had to get enough dried meat and pemmican to last all winter. At this time the buffalo would be fat and the calves grown up. Calves were not killed as no one cared for veal anyway.

The homeward journey was slow, but who cared? The nice sunny days in the fall, Indian summer, made travelling rather fascinating. Occasionally we would run into bad weather, but we were accustomed to it and did not mind as long as we had plenty of the best and most nourishing food I ever ate. In all, I made four trips to the plains hunting the buffalo. Each was further away toward south.

Bibliography

Alward, Mary M. "Victoria Callihoo." *Canadian Tourism*. June 23, 2001.

Anderson, Anne. *The First Métis: A New Nation*. Edmonton: UVISCO Press, 1985.

Bakker, Peter. *A Language of Our Own: The Genesis of Michif, the Mixed Cree-French Language of the Canadian Métis*. Oxford University Press, 1997.

Barkwell, Lawrence J., Leah Dorion, and Darren R. Prefontaine. *Resources for Métis Researchers*. Winnipeg: Gabriel Dumont Institute and Manitoba Métis Federation, 1999.

Belcourt, Herb. *Walking in the Woods: A Métis Journey*. Edmonton: Brindle & Glass Publishing, 2006.

Brink, Jack W. *Imagining Head-Smashed-In: Aboriginal Buffalo Hunting on the Northern Plains.* Edmonton: Athabasca University Press, 2008.

Callihoo, Victoria. "Early Life in Lac Ste. Anne and St. Albert in the 1870s." *Alberta Historical Review,* Vol. 1, No. 3, 1953.

—"Our Buffalo Hunts," In *Alberta Historical Review.* Vol. 8, No. 1, 1960.

—"The Iroquois in Alberta," In *Alberta Historical Review,* Vol. 7, No. 2, 1959.

Carnegie, James. "The Earl of Southesk." in *Saskatchewan and the Rocky Mountains: A Diary and Narrative of Travel, Sport and Adventure during a Journey through the Hudson's Bay Company Territories in 1859 and 1860.* Edmonton: Hurtig Publishing, 1969.

"Centenarian Dies in St. Albert Home." *Edmonton Journal,* April 22, 1966.

Chalmers, John W. "Treaty No. 6." *Alberta History.* Vol. 25, No. 2, 1977.

Cheadle, Walter B. *Cheadle's Journal of a Trip Across Canada 1862–1863.* Edmonton: Hurtig Publishing, 1971.

Chodin, Tim, and Dan Asfar. *Gabriel Dumont: War Leader of the Métis.* Edmonton: Folklore Publishing, 2003.

Cruise, David, and Allison Griffiths. *The Great Adventure.* Penguin Canada, 1998.

Drouin, Emeric, OMI. *Lac Ste. Anne Sakahigan.* Edmonton: Editions de L'Ermitage, 1973.

Ellis, Eleanor. *Northern Cookbook.* Ottawa: Indian Affairs and Northern Development, 1967.

Foster, J.E. "End of the Plains Buffalo." *Buffalo.* Vol. 3, No. 1, 1992.

Harper's Bazaar excerpt, October 1860. Taken from Manitoba Historical Society: http://www.mhs.mb.ca/docs/pageant/07/redriverjig.shtml

Hollihan, Tony. *Kootenai Brown.* Edmonton: Folklore Publishing, 2001.

Lac Ste. Anne Historical Society, *West of the Fifth* [Local History]. Edmonton: Institute of Applied Art, 1959.

MacDonald, Janice E. *The Northwest Fort: Fort Edmonton.* Edmonton: Lone Pine Publishing, 1983.

MacEwan, Grant. "Victoria Callihoo: Granny." *And Mighty Women Too: Stories of Western Canadian Pioneers.* Saskatoon: Prairie Books, 1975.

MacGregor, J.G. *John Rowand: Czar of the Prairies.* Saskatoon: Prairie Books, 1978.

—*Overland by the Yellowhead*. Saskatoon: Prairie Books, 1974.

Macpherson, Elizabeth. *The Sun Traveller: The Story of the Callihoos in Alberta*. St. Albert, AB: Musée Héritage Museum, 2003.

Newman, Peter C. *Caesars of the Wilderness*. Canada: Viking/Penguin Books, 1987.

Nicks, Trudy. "Missions Impossible," taken from: http://archiver.rootsweb.ancestry.com/th/read/METISGEN/2002-03/1015532508

Racette, Sherry Farrell. *The Flower Beadwork People*. Saskatoon: Gabriel Dumont Institute, 1991.

Simon, Steven. *Healing Waters*. Edmonton: University of Alberta Press, 1995.

Stenson, Fred. *The Trade*. Vancouver: Douglas & McIntyre, 2000.

Strasbourg, Alvena (Laboucane). *Memories of a Métis Woman*. Self-published, 1997.

Taylor, Cora. "Buffalo Hunters of Tail Creek." *Celebrating Alberta: Many Places*. Don Mills, ON: Pearson Education Canada, 2007.

—*Angelique: Book One—The Buffalo Hunt*. Penguin Canada, 2002.

Tellenius, Clarence. "An Artist Among the Buffalo." *Buffalo*. Vol. 3, No. 1, 1992.

Van Kirk, Sylvia. *Many Tender Ties: Women in the Fur Trade Society*. University of Oklahoma Press, 1980.

Verbicky-Todd, Eleanor. *Buffalo Hunting Among the Plains Indians*. Occasional Paper #24, Alberta Culture, 1984.

Woodcock, George. *Gabriel Dumont: The Métis Chief and His Lost World*. Edmonton: Hurtig Publishers, 1975.

Wright, Milt. "This Chip's for You Too." *Buffalo*. Vol. 3, No. 1, 1992.

Web Sources

"A Few Thoughts About Red River Carts." Clay County Historical Society Newsletter, March/April 2000. http://www.info.co.clay.mn.us/history/red_river_carts.htm

Alberta Online Encyclopedia:

www.albertasource.ca/metis/eng/people_and_communities/tail_creek_callihoo.htm

Aboriginal Multi-Media Society of Alberta (AMMSA), Buffalo Spirit, Footprints, Victoria Belcourt Callihoo: www.ammsa.com/buffalospirit/2004/footprints-VBCallihoo.html

Lac Ste. Anne Pilgrimage: www.lsap.ca

"Canadians Fastest to Cross Antarctica." January 8, 2009: http://www.edmontonjournal.com/Canadians+fastest+cross+Antarctica/1154271/story.htm

Cooper, Wayne. "The Battle of Round Mountain—November 19, 1861." Art of the Oklahoma State Capitol:

www.ok.gov/~arts/capitolart/permart/paintings/wcooper/roundmountain.html

Indian Claims Commission Report:

http://www.indianclaims.ca/media/news-en.asp?id=232&content_type=2

"Interview with Yvonne [Chartrand] about the Red River Jig." Compaigni V'ni Dansi. www.vnidansi.ca/resources/interview-with-yvonne-about-the-red-river-jig

Library and Archives of Canada—Women's Exhibition—Celebrating Women's Achievements—Victoria Belcourt Callihoo—Métis Historian:

http://www.collectionscanada.gc.ca/women/002026-203-e.html

The Métis in Alberta, "Buffalo Lake and Tail Creek":

http://www.albertasource.ca/METIS/eng/people_and_communities/historic_buffalo_lake.htm

The Métis in Alberta, "The People of Tail Creek":

http://www.albertasource.ca/METIS/eng/people_and_communities/tail_creek-people.htm

Métis Culture and Heritage Resource Centre—Red River Cart Building:

http://www.metisresourcecentre.mb.ca/history/rrcartb.htm

Métis Nation—Heritage Canada: www.metisnation.ca

Prefontaine, Darren R., Todd Paquin, and Patrick Young. "Traditional Métis Transportation."

http://www.metismuseum.ca/media/document.php/00728.pdf

"Red River Cart" entry, The Encyclopedia of Saskatchewan: http://esask.uregina.ca/entry/red_river_cart.html

Other Sources

Lund, Carrielynn. Communication with the author October 10, 2007.

MacDonald, Janice. Communication with the author February 20, 2007.

McIlwraith, Naomi. Communication with the author February 2, 2009.

Musée Héritage Museum, St. Albert, AB—Descendant Report, Métis Genealogical Records.

Oblates of Mary Immaculate, Records of the Order. xiv Registres de baptemes, Mariages et Sepultres Fort des Prairies. 1842–1888. 71.220/5213-5217. Provincial Archives of Alberta.

Papen, Robert A. Communication with the author February 11, 2009.

Patterson, Frieda. Telephone conversation with the author, January 10, 2009.

Index

ABC

DEF

OPQ

RST

Cora Taylor

AWARD-WINNING AND BESTSELLING author and writing advocate, Cora Taylor, is the author of more than 20 other books, many for young adults. She has won three major children's literature prizes, including the Canada Council Children's Literature Prize, and her books have been adopted for use with provincial curricula. She has held the post of National President of the Canadian Authors Associations, President of the CAA Fund to Develop Canadian Writers as well as many other executive positions in the Canadian writers' world.

She has always had an abiding interest and pride in her Métis heritage and many of the books she writes describe the day-to-day lives of early Canadians. She based the character of Angelique from her popular Our Canadian Girl series on the life of Victoria Callihoo.